THE HISTORIC TAX CREDIT

A Practitioner's Guide to the Technical Tax Issues

Second Edition

WILLIAM F. MACHEN

AMERICAN BAR ASSOCIATION

Forum on Affordable Housing and Community Development

Cover design by Carolina Martinez/ABA Design

Printed in the United States of America.

27 26 25 24 23 5 4 3 2 1

ISBN 978-1-63905-392-6

Discounts are available for books ordered in bulk. Special consideration is given to state bars, CLE programs, and other bar-related organizations. Inquire at Book Publishing, ABA Publishing, American Bar Association, 321 N. Clark Street, Chicago, Illinois 60654–7598.

www.shopABA.org

The author would like to dedicate this book to his wife, Leslie, his son, Scott, and his daughter, Kaitlin, her husband, Tyson, and their two children, Nolan and Austin.

Contents

Chapter One

Introduction

1.1 OVERVIEW

The federal rehabilitation tax credit described in Internal Revenue Code § 47 (Historic Tax Credit) has been one of the most effective tools available in recent years for preserving historic buildings and other resources in the United States, as well as revitalizing many of our communities and spurring economic growth.[1] Implementing a plan to effectively utilize this tool is challenging due to the complexity of many of the applicable statutory and regulatory provisions and the frequent need to integrate such provisions with other federal, state, and local community development incentives.

This book introduces the reader both to the basic rules relating to how the Historic Tax Credit works and to some of the technical complexities that arise in structuring transactions involving this powerful tax incentive.

Most large historic rehabilitation projects are owned by limited partnerships or limited liability companies (LLCs) formed by a developer for the purpose of attracting capital investments from investors who are able to utilize the Historic Tax Credits generated by the rehabilitation. In some cases, a single corporate or institutional investor is admitted to the limited partnership or LLC as a limited partner or investor member. In other cases, a third party syndicator assembles a group of investors who pool their capital and invest in the ownership entity through a separate limited partnership or LLC. For the sake of simplicity, any such structured tax equity investment will be referred to herein as a "syndicated" transaction, whether or not a separate syndication company is involved.

1 According to a study prepared by Rutgers University, properties financed by equity from the Historic Tax Credit generated 135,000 jobs and $8 billion in total rehabilitation investment in 2021. The jobs total was up 10.6 percent and the investment total was up 9.5 percent over the reported 2020 totals. The National Park Service certified 1,063 completed historic rehabilitation projects in fiscal year 2021 and approved another 1,098 proposed projects. According to the report, 44 percent of the projects in 2021 were in low- and moderate-income census tracts and 78 percent were in economically distressed areas. The report states that the Historic Tax Credit has produced more than 3 million jobs since 1979 and has led to an additional $60.7 billion in federal, state and local taxes. *See* Rutgers Univ., Annual Report on the Economic Impact of the Federal Historic Tax Credit for 2021, http://www.nps.gov/tps/tax-incentives/taxdocs/economic-impact-2021.pdf.

1.2 LEGISLATIVE BACKGROUND

1.2.1 Statutory Provisions

Code § 38(b)(1) provides that the current year general business credit includes the investment credit determined under Code § 46. The investment credit under Code § 46 includes the Historic Tax Credit under Code § 47.

Former Code § 47 was substantially revised in 2017 by section 13402 of the Tax Cuts and Jobs Act (TCJA). Prior to the TCJA, Code § 47(a) provided for the purposes of Code § 46 a two-tier credit for qualified rehabilitation expenditures (QREs) incurred in connection with the rehabilitation of a "qualified rehabilitated building." The pre-TCJA version of Code § 47(a)(2) allowed a 20 percent credit for QREs with respect to a "certified historic structure," and Code § 47(a)(1) allowed a 10 percent credit for QREs with respect to a qualified rehabilitated building other than a certified historic structure (for certain buildings first placed in service before 1936, "pre-1936 buildings"). Both the 20 percent and 10 percent credits were fully allowed in the taxable year the qualified rehabilitated building was placed in service.

The TCJA repealed the 10 percent credit for pre-1936 buildings and modified the rules for claiming the 20 percent credit for certified historic structures.[2] The TCJA also amended Code § 47(c), in part, by re-designating former Code § 47(c)(1)(C) and (D) as Code § 47(c)(1)(B) and (C).[3] These amendments generally were applicable to QREs paid or incurred after December 31, 2017, subject to a statutory transition rule (TCJA Transition Rule).[4]

As discussed herein, the Code currently provides that, for the purposes of Code § 46, for any taxable year during the five-year period beginning in the taxable year in which a qualified rehabilitated building is placed in service, the Historic Tax Credit for such year is an amount equal to the "ratable share" for such year.[5]

Code § 47(a)(2) defines the ratable share for any taxable year during the five-year period described in Code § 47(a)(1) as an amount equal to 20 percent of the QREs with respect to the qualified rehabilitated building, as allocated ratably to each year during the five-year period.

QREs with respect to any qualified rehabilitated building are taken into account for the taxable year in which the qualified rehabilitated building is placed in service. However, as noted earlier, the Historic Tax Credit attributable to such QREs is taken ratably over the five-year period beginning with the placed-in-service year.[6]

2 TCJA § 13402(a).
3 *Id.* § 13402(b).
4 *Id.* § 13402(c)(2).
5 I.R.C. § 47(a)(1).
6 *Id.* § 47(b).

A qualified rehabilitated building must be a building that has been substantially rehabilitated.[7] A building is treated as substantially rehabilitated only if the QREs incurred during the 24-month period selected by the taxpayer ending with or within the taxable year exceed the greater of the taxpayer's adjusted basis in the building (and its structural components) or $5,000.[8] For certain rehabilitations expected to be completed in phases set forth in architectural plans and specifications completed before the rehabilitation begins (i.e., a phased rehabilitation), the taxpayer may select a 60-month period rather than a 24-month period.[9]

The TCJA Transition Rule provided that in the case of QREs (for either a certified historic structure eligible for a 20 percent credit or a pre-1936 building eligible for a 10 percent credit prior to December 31, 2017), with respect to any building owned or leased by the taxpayer at all times on and after January 1, 2018, the 24-month period selected by the taxpayer under Code § 47(c)(1)(B)(i) or the 60-month period selected by the taxpayer under the rule for a phased rehabilitation under Code § 47(c)(1)(B)(ii) is to begin no later than the end of the 180-day period beginning on December 22, 2017, and the amendments made by section 13402 of the TCJA apply to such QREs paid or incurred after the end of the taxable year in which such 24-month or 60-month period ends. For taxpayers selecting a 24-month period, the requirement to begin the period within 180 days from December 22, 2017, meant that the latest day that such a 24-month period can end under the TCJA Transition Rule was June 20, 2020. For taxpayers permitted to select a 60-month period for a phased rehabilitation, the requirement to begin the period within 180 days from December 22, 2017, meant that the latest day that such a 60-month period could end under the TCJA Transition Rule was June 20, 2023.[10]

1.2.2 What Is a Certified Rehabilitation of a Certified Historic Structure?

A certified historic structure is a building that either is listed as such in the National Register of Historic Places (National Register) or is located in a "registered historic district" and is certified by the Secretary of the Interior (Secretary), acting through the National Park Service (NPS), as being of historic significance to the district.[11] A registered historic district includes any district listed in the National Register, as well as a district statutorily designated by a

7 *Id.* § 47(c)(1)(A)(i).

8 *Id.* § 47(c)(1)(B)(i).

9 *Id.* § 47(c)(1)(B)(ii); Treas. Reg. § 1.48-12(b)(2)(v).

10 *See* Section 2.1 for a discussion of certain extensions of such time periods granted as relief in response to the COVID-19 pandemic.

11 I.R.C. § 47(c)(3)(A).

state or local government, provided that the relevant statute has been certified by the Secretary as incorporating proper criteria for substantially achieving the purpose of preserving and rehabilitating historically significant buildings, and the district is certified by the Secretary as satisfying substantially all of the requirements for the listing of districts in the National Register.[12]

As already noted, in order to be eligible for the Historic Tax Credit, the building must be a "qualified rehabilitated building," which the Code defines as a building (including its structural components) for which depreciation (or amortization in lieu of depreciation) is allowable that has been "substantially rehabilitated," as discussed later, and that was placed in service before the beginning of the rehabilitation. In addition, prior to the passage of the TCJA, if the building was not a certified historic structure (and thus qualified only for the 10 percent credit), the rehabilitation had to satisfy certain external wall and internal structural framework conditions.[13] The term "building" is not defined in Code § 47. The old investment credit regulations contained a fairly comprehensive definition of "building" for purposes of defining "section 38 property."[14] Presumably, the same (or a substantially similar) definition applies today to determine what is a "building" for purposes of the Historic Tax Credit.

---

12 *Id.* § 47(c)(3)(B).

13 *Id.* § 47(c)(1)(A)–(B), prior to the amendments contained in the TCJA.

14 Treas. Reg. § 1.48-1(e)(1). Treas. Reg. §§ 1.48-1 to 1.48-12 cited herein were issued under Former Code § 48, which was repealed by Pub. L. No. 101-508, 104 Stat. 1388-1, 536–59 (1990). Treas. Reg. § 1.48-1(e)(1) provides:

> Generally, buildings and structural components thereof do not qualify as section 38 property. See, however, section 48(a)(1)(E) and (g), and § 1.48-11 (relating to investment credit for qualified rehabilitated building). The term "building" generally means any structure or edifice enclosing a space within its walls, and usually covered by a roof, the purpose of which is, for example, to provide shelter or housing, or to provide working, office, parking, display, or sales space. The term includes, for example, structures such as apartment houses, factory and office buildings, warehouses, barns, garages, railway or bus stations, and stores. Such term includes any such structure constructed by, or for, a lessee even if such structure must be removed, or ownership of such structure reverts to the lessor, at the termination of the lease. Such term does not include (i) a structure which is essentially an item of machinery or equipment, or (ii) a structure which houses property used as an integral part of an activity specified in I.R.C. § 48(a)(1)(B)(i) if the use of the structure is so closely related to the use of such property that the structure clearly can be expected to be replaced when the property it initially houses is replaced. Factors which indicate that a structure is closely related to the use of the property it houses include the fact that the structure is specifically designated to provide for the stress and other demands of such property and the fact that the structure could not be economically used for other purposes. Thus, the term "building" does not include such structures as oil and gas storage tanks, grain storage bins, silos, fractionating towers, blast furnaces, basic oxygen furnaces, coke ovens, brick kilns, and coal tipples.

As discussed later, the basis of property for which the Historic Tax Credit is claimed must be reduced by the amount of the credit. Similarly, as discussed in Chapter Eight, a partner in a partnership that has claimed the Historic Tax Credit must reduce both its capital account and its basis for its interest in the partnership by the amount of the credit.[15]

As a general matter, there are no limitations on how a building eligible for the Historic Tax Credit is maintained or operated, although the availability of the credit is subject to the lodging facility rule set forth in Code § 50(b)(2). Subject to certain exceptions, this rule makes property used predominantly to furnish lodging or in connection with the furnishing of lodging ineligible for an investment credit such as the Historic Tax Credit. However, this limitation does not apply to a certified historic structure to the extent of the portion of basis that is attributable to QREs.[16] Moreover, property operated as a hotel or motel in which the predominant portion of the accommodations is used by transients also qualifies for the Historic Tax Credit.[17] As discussed in Chapter Seven, various limitations apply to the use of the Historic Tax Credit where the rehabilitation improvements are used by or leased to governmental entities, tax-exempt entities, or foreign persons.[18]

In order for a rehabilitation to constitute a certified rehabilitation of a certified historic structure, a complex approval process involving the applicable state housing preservation officer (SHPO), the NPS, and the Internal Revenue Service (IRS) is involved.

The treasury regulations define a certified rehabilitation as:

> any rehabilitation of a certified historic structure that the Secretary of the Interior has certified to the Internal Revenue Service as being consistent with the historic character of the building and, where applicable, the district in which such building is located. The determination of the scope of a rehabilitation shall be made on the basis of all the facts and circumstances surrounding the rehabilitation and shall not be made solely on the basis of ownership. The Secretary of the Interior shall take all of the rehabilitation work performed as part of a single rehabilitation, including any post-certification work, into account in determining whether the rehabilitation complies with the Department of Interior standards for rehabilitation and whether the certification should be granted, revoked, or otherwise invalidated.[19]

---

15 *See* Section 8.2.

16 I.R.C. § 50(b)(2)(C). Since under current law a qualified rehabilitated building must be a certified historic structure to be eligible for the credit, the lodging exception no longer has any particular relevance. See Chapter Six.

17 *Id.* § 50(b)(2)(B).

18 *See* Section 7.2.

19 Treas. Reg. § 1.48-12(d)(3).

To initiate the certified rehabilitation process, the owner of the building must complete an historic preservation certification application and submit it to the SHPO for the state in which the building is located. The SHPO reviews the application and forwards it to the NPS, generally with a recommendation as to whether it should be approved. While the recommendations of the SHPO normally are accepted by the NPS, that is not always the case, and all final certification decisions are made by the NPS.

Part 1 of the historic preservation application is used for the following purposes:

(i) to request certification that a depreciable building contributes to the significance of a registered historic district and therefore qualifies as a certified historic structure for the purpose of rehabilitation;
(ii) to request certification that a depreciable or non-depreciable structure or building, and, where appropriate, the land area on which such a structure or building is located, contributes to the significance of the registered historic district in which it is located, for a charitable contribution for conservation purposes;
(iii) to request certification that a building does not contribute to the significance of the registered historic district in which it is located;
(iv) to request a preliminary determination of whether an individual building not yet on the National Register meets the National Register Criteria for Evaluation and will likely be listed in the National Register when nominated according to the procedures set forth in 36 C.F.R. Part 60;
(v) to request a preliminary determination that a building located within a potential historic district contributes to the significance of the district; and
(vi) to request a preliminary determination that a building outside the period or area of significance of a registered historic district contributes to the significance of the district.

If the building is individually listed in the National Register, the owner normally is not required to complete Part 1 of the application. However, if the project contains more than one building, the owner must submit a single Part 1 application that describes all the buildings in the listing. Moreover, the owner of a building that is not yet listed in the National Register, or that is located within a potential historic district, may request a preliminary determination from the NPS as to whether such building may qualify as a certified historic structure when the building or the district is listed in the National Register. Preliminary determinations also may be requested for buildings outside the period or area of significance of a registered historic district.

Part 2 of the historic preservation application requires the owner to provide certain basic information concerning the building(s) and to describe in detail the rehabilitation work to be undertaken with respect to the building(s). This description must cover the entire project and not just those portions that are expected to qualify for the Historic Tax Credit. If the nature or scope of the project changes after the initial application has been submitted, the owner must submit to the NPS a continuation/amendment sheet describing such changes. In order to qualify for the Historic Tax Credit, the proposed rehabilitation work must satisfy the Secretary's Standards for Rehabilitation. The Guidelines for Rehabilitating Historic Buildings accompanying the Standards provide further guidance to owners.

Parts 1 and 2 of the historic preservation application may be completed and submitted separately or together. However, if the two are sent separately, Part 1 must be submitted first. Unless the building already is individually listed in the National Register, Part 2 will not be processed until an adequately documented Part 1 has been submitted and acted upon.

A project does not become a certified rehabilitation eligible for the Historic Tax Credit until it has been completed and so designated by the NPS. When the rehabilitation work has been completed, the owner must complete a Request for Certification of Completed Work and submit it to the SHPO. The completed project may be inspected by an authorized representative of the Secretary to confirm that the work conforms to the Standards for Rehabilitation. The final approval by the NPS of the completed project commonly is referred to as "Part 3 approval."

Prior to passage of the TCJA, the Historic Tax Credit normally was available in the year in which the property generating the credit (i.e., the rehabilitation improvements funded with the QREs) was "placed in service." As noted earlier, the credit is now claimed ratably over a five-year period. If such property is sold or otherwise disposed of within a five-year period following the placed-in-service date, all or a portion of the credit is required to be recaptured.[20]

Ordinarily, the Historic Tax Credit is claimed by the owner of the property generating the credit. Under certain circumstances, however, the credit may be claimed by a lessee of such property. Such lease structures present a series of technical issues that do not arise in the case of direct ownership.[21]

Many older or historic buildings are owned by limited partnerships or LLCs that seek to attract capital by allocating the benefits of the Historic Tax Credit to one or more investors. Because of the limitations on the use of credits and losses from passive activities, the vast majority of these investors are widely held corporations. While the dollars invested in historic rehabilitation projects dramatically increased in recent years, the decision of the Third Circuit in the *Historic Boardwalk Hall*[22] case in 2012 called into question many long-standing structuring practices in syndicated Historic Tax Credit transactions and caused a temporary decrease in investor interest in such investments.

20 *See* Section 10.1.

21 *See* Chapter Nine.

22 Historic Boardwalk Hall, LLC, et al. v. Comm'r of Internal Revenue, 694 F.3d 425 (3d Cir. 2012).

The *Historic Boardwalk* decision, and the issuance by the IRS of Rev. Proc. 2014-12 in response to the market dislocation caused by such decision, are discussed in more detail in Chapter Twelve.

A sponsor or investor seeking to avail itself of the benefits of the Historic Tax Credit must be familiar with a number of complex tax issues. To complicate matters even further, in 1990, Congress renumbered and eliminated several Code sections relating to tax credits. Currently, Code § 47 contains most of the provisions relating to the Historic Tax Credit, but the discussion that follows will refer to some Code sections in effect prior to 1990, and in some cases to sections of the Internal Revenue Code of 1954. Those sections will be referred to herein as "Former" Code sections. In particular, Code § 48 now relates to energy credits, but Former Code § 48 and the related treasury regulations thereunder contained the rules governing an election to treat a lessee as the purchaser of rehabilitation improvements generating an Historic Tax Credit.[23] These rules are now incorporated by reference in Code § 50(d).[24]

23 Treas. Reg. § 1.48-4, -12.

24 I.R.C. § 50(d)(5).

Chapter Two

The Substantial Rehabilitation Test

2.1 SUBSTANTIAL REHABILITATION TEST

In order to be eligible for the Historic Tax Credit, a building must be a qualified rehabilitated building. The Code defines the term "qualified rehabilitated building" to mean any building (and its structural components) that satisfies the following requirements:

(i) the building has been substantially rehabilitated (as described in this section);
(ii) the building was placed in service before the beginning of the rehabilitation;
(iii) such building is a certified historic structure; and
(iv) depreciation (or amortization in lieu of depreciation) is allowable with respect to such property.[1]

A building generally will be treated as having been substantially rehabilitated if the QREs incurred during the 24-month (or, in some cases, 60-month) period selected by the taxpayer and ending with or within the taxable year exceed the greater of $5,000 or the adjusted basis of the building and its structural components, determined as of the beginning of the first day of the 24-month (or 60-month, as applicable) period or the holding period of the building, whichever is later.[2] Congress has provided exceptions to strict compliance with the 24-month (or 60-month, as applicable) rule in the case of taxpayers affected by presidentially declared disasters or terrorist or military actions.[3] Code § 7508A provides the Secretary of the Treasury or his or her delegate with authority to postpone the time for performing certain acts under the internal revenue laws for a taxpayer determined by the Secretary of the Treasury to be affected by a federally declared disaster as defined in Code § 165(i)(5)(A). Pursuant to

1 I.R.C. § 47(c)(1)(A).

2 *Id.* § 47(c)(1)(B). *See* Chapter Six for a discussion of the types of expenditures that are included in the definition of "qualified rehabilitation expenditures."

3 I.R.C. § 7508A; Treas. Reg. § 301.7508A-1.

Code § 7508A(a), a period of up to one year may be disregarded in determining whether the performance of certain acts is timely under the internal revenue laws.

On March 13, 2020, the President issued an emergency declaration (Notice 2020-58) under the Stafford Act in response to the ongoing Coronavirus Disease 2019 (COVID-19) pandemic. The emergency declaration instructed the Secretary of the Treasury "to provide relief from tax deadlines to Americans who have been adversely affected by the COVID-19 emergency, as appropriate, pursuant to 26 U.S.C. 7508A(a)." Section III of the notice described the relief provided pursuant to Code § 7508A(a) for certain requirements of the Historic Tax Credit. Under Section III, for purposes of Code § 47(c)(1)(B) and Treas. Reg. § 1.48-12(b)(2), if the 24- or 60-month measuring period in which the requisite amount of QREs have to be paid or incurred in order to satisfy the substantial rehabilitation test for a building originally ended on or after April 1, 2020, and before March 31, 2021, the last day of the 24- or 60-month measuring period for a taxpayer to incur the requisite QREs with respect to the building was postponed to March 31, 2021. This meant that a taxpayer could have a measuring period that was longer than 24 or 60 months.

In addition, for purposes of taxpayers subject to the TCJA Transition Rule, if the 24- or 60-month measuring period in which the requisite amount of QREs had to be paid or incurred in order to satisfy the substantial rehabilitation test for a building originally ended on or after April 1, 2020, and before March 31, 2021, the last day of the 24- or 60-month measuring period for a taxpayer to pay or incur the requisite QREs with respect to the building was postponed to March 31, 2021. Thus, if the requisite QREs described in the preceding sentence were paid or incurred by March 31, 2021, the TCJA Transition Rule permitted the rules of Former Code § 47 allowing the 10 percent and 20 percent credits in a single year to apply to QREs paid or incurred with respect to such building in the taxable year in which the 24- or 60-month measuring period (the last day of which was postponed by this notice) ended. In addition, the amendments made by section 13402(a) and (b) of the TCJA, under which only the 20 percent credit is allowed over five years, would apply to QREs paid or incurred with respect to such building in succeeding taxable years.

On April 9, 2020, the Department of the Treasury and the IRS issued Notice 2020-23, 2020-18 I.R.B. 742, which pursuant to Code § 7508A provided certain relief to affected taxpayers and postponed due dates until July 15, 2020, with respect to certain tax filings and payments, certain time-sensitive government actions, and all time-sensitive actions listed in Rev. Proc. 2018-58, 2018-50 I.R.B. 990 (December 10, 2018) that were due to be performed on or after April 1, 2020, and before July 15, 2020.[4] Among the relief granted, Notice 2020-23

4 *See* Notice 2020-23 and Rev. Proc. 2018-58.

(referencing Rev. Proc. 2018-58) postponed until July 15, 2020, the time to perform certain time-sensitive actions for purposes of Code § 47 that were due to be performed on or after April 1, 2020, and before July 15, 2020, including the time period for satisfying the substantial rehabilitation test described in Former Code § 47(c)(1)(C) (re-designated as Code § 47(c)(1)(B) by the TCJA) and Treas. Reg. § 1.48-12(b)(2).

The 24-month (or 60-month, as applicable) measuring period also can be extended for purposes of a substantial rehabilitation by individuals serving in the U.S. Armed Forces, or in support of the U.S. Armed Forces, in a combat zone.[5]

For purposes of satisfying the substantial rehabilitation test, a taxpayer is permitted to take into account QREs incurred during the same rehabilitation process by any other person having an interest in the building.[6] For example, a lessee may include the expenditures of the lessor for purposes of applying the substantial rehabilitation test. Note, however, that for purposes of applying the test, the "adjusted basis of the building and its structural components" means the *aggregate* adjusted basis in the building (and its structural components) of *all* parties having an interest in the building. By way of illustration, if a building is divided into separate condominium units, it would be necessary to compare the QREs incurred by all of the condominium unit owners (including expenses incurred by any lessees) to the adjusted basis of all such unit owners (including the basis of any such lessees in their leasehold interests and leasehold improvements) in the building (and its structural components).

2.2 HOW TO SATISFY THE TEST

As discussed previously, there are two ways to satisfy the substantial rehabilitation test.

The first way is to comply with the 24-month rule described in Section 2.1. Under this rule, a simple mathematical determination is required as to whether the expenditures incurred during the applicable 24-month period satisfy the mathematical test.

The second way is to comply with a special 60-month phased rehabilitation rule.[7] For this rule to apply, the taxpayer must obtain architectural plans and specifications *before* beginning the rehabilitation that show that the rehabilitation is expected to take place in phases. This rule permits the taxpayer to look back 60 months (rather than 24 months) prior to the placed-in-service date (or the last day of the measuring period selected by the taxpayer in the year the building is placed in service) to see if the mathematical test has been satisfied. Like the 24-month measuring period, the 60-month measuring period may be

5 I.R.C. § 7508(a).

6 Treas. Reg. § 1.48-12(b)(2)(vi); Priv. Ltr. Rul. 8639026 (June 26, 1986).

7 I.R.C. § 47(c)(1)(B)(ii).

extended in the case of rehabilitations undertaken by military personnel in a combat zone or in situations involving disasters, terrorist actions, or military operations.[8]

Fortunately, the treasury regulations adopt a liberal interpretation of the requirement that a phased rehabilitation be described in "architectural plans and specifications completed before the rehabilitation begins." The treasury regulations provide that "written plans that describe generally all phases of the rehabilitation process shall be treated as written architectural plans and specifications. Such written plans are not required to contain detailed working drawings or detailed specifications of the materials to be used. In addition, the taxpayer may include a description of work to be done by lessees in the written plans."[9]

It is important to understand that the 60-month phased rehabilitation rule does not apply when a rehabilitation *unexpectedly* becomes a phased project. It applies only where the rehabilitation may "reasonably be expected to be completed in phases" as evidenced by architectural plans and specifications.[10] Therefore, in any instance where a rehabilitation may be completed in phases, the developer should make sure that written plans complying with the regulatory requirements described here exist prior to the beginning of the rehabilitation work in order to take advantage of the 60-month rule if necessary.

The treasury regulations provide that a phased rehabilitation must consist of two or more distinct stages of development, the determination of which shall be made on the basis of all relevant facts and circumstances.[11] The regulations do not require that the rehabilitation period must exceed 24 months nor do they provide a clear definition of what qualifies as a distinct stage of development. There also is no application or approval process for a project to qualify as a phased rehabilitation.

There are a number of situations where the phased rehabilitation rule will be beneficial. The most obvious is when a large project is expected to take longer than the basic 24-month measuring period. Similarly, if a rehabilitation does not include an entire building and the developer is planning to rehabilitate distinct portions of the building at separate times, the 60-month rule can significantly increase the QREs eligible for the credit. The rule also can be useful in a project where the NPS considers multiple buildings to be functionally related historically and treated as a single certified historic structure. The NPS rules relating to functionally related buildings are discussed in detail in Chapter Five.[12]

The phased rehabilitation rule gained more prominence as a result of the extension of time granted under Notice 2020-58 to satisfy the TCJA Transition

---

8 *See* Section 2.1.

9 Treas. Reg. § 1.48-12(b)(2)(v); Priv. Ltr. Rul. 8639026 (June 26, 1986).

10 I.R.C. § 47(c)(1)(C)(ii).

11 Treas. Reg. § 1.48-12(b)(2)(v).

12 *See* Section 5.2.

Rule. For years 2022 and 2023, only projects that qualified as phased rehabilitations could satisfy the TCJA Transition Rule and qualify for the pre-TCJA one-year Historic Tax Credit.

Regardless of which of the substantial rehabilitation rules applies, it should be noted that as long as the applicable test is satisfied, the Historic Tax Credit is available not just with respect to the QREs incurred during the 24-month or 60-month measuring period but also with respect to all QREs incurred prior to the measuring period, so long as they were part of the same substantial rehabilitation, and to all QREs incurred after the measuring period but before the last day of the tax year in which the measuring period ends.[13]

13 Treas. Reg. § 1.48-12(c)(6).

Chapter Three

Placed-in-Service and Timing Rules

3.1 WHEN ARE REHABILITATION IMPROVEMENTS PLACED IN SERVICE?

The Historic Tax Credit generally is available ratably over a five-year period commencing in the taxable year in which the property generating the credit is placed in service by the taxpayer. The treasury regulations provide that property is placed in service for this purpose on the *earlier* of (i) the taxable year in which, under the taxpayer's depreciation practices, depreciation commences, or (ii) the taxable year in which the property is placed in a condition or state of readiness and availability for its assigned function.[1] Similarly, the treasury regulations state, in relevant part, that "[t]he investment credit for qualified rehabilitation expenditures is generally allowed in the taxable year in which the property attributable to the expenditure is placed in service, provided the building is a qualified rehabilitated building for the taxable year."[2]

The treasury regulations make it clear that, as long as the building constitutes a qualified rehabilitated building, the test is not when the building is placed in service but when the improvements attributable to the QREs are placed in service.[3] In a so-called "rolling rehab," where the historic building is rehabilitated

1 Treas. Reg. § 1.46-3(d).

2 *Id.* § 1.48-12(f)(2)(i). Note that the IRS has taken the position that the issuance of a certificate of occupancy is not conclusive evidence that property has been placed in service. *See, e.g.*, Priv. Ltr. Ruls. 9243032, 9146017, and 9120021; TAM 8415003, and Notice 88-116.

3 Treas. Reg. § 1.48-12(f)(2)(ii) provides:

> Section 38 property described in I.R.C. § 48(a)(1)(E). In the case of section 38 property described in I.R.C. § 48(a)(1)(E), the section 38 property is not the building. Instead, the section 38 property is the portion of the basis of the building that is attributable to qualified rehabilitation expenditures. Therefore, for example, for purposes of the determination of when such section 38 property is placed in service, a determination must be made regarding when property attributable to the portion of the basis of the building attributable to qualified rehabilitation expenditures is placed in service. The issue of when the building is placed in service is thus not relevant.

with tenants in place, the rehabilitation improvements will be deemed to be placed in service in the first taxable year in which the building constitutes a qualified rehabilitated building.[4]

Notwithstanding the foregoing general rules, the treasury regulations provide a special placed-in-service rule that applies to leasing transactions involving an election to treat the lessee as the purchaser of the rehabilitation improvements under Former Code § 48(d), which is incorporated by reference in current Code § 50(d).[5] Specifically, the treasury regulations state:

> (3) Notwithstanding subparagraph (1) of this paragraph, property with respect to which an election is made under Code § 1.48-4 to treat the lessee as having purchased such property shall be considered placed in service by the lessor in the taxable year in which possession is transferred to such lessee.[6]

This special rule has been cited in several cases. For example, in *Garcia*,[7] a case involving a master recording limited partnership, the taxpayers argued that the valuation overstatement rules of Former Code § 6659 did not apply because the master recording at issue was not placed in service until 1984, when records were first produced from the master, thus disqualifying the master for the investment credit. The Tax Court rejected this argument, observing that because an election under Former Code § 48(d) had been executed with respect

---

> In fact, under this test, the building itself may never have been taken out of service during the rehabilitation process. If the building is rehabilitated over several years in stages (e.g., by floors), section 38 property attributable to qualified rehabilitation expenditures to a qualified rehabilitated building placed in service in each taxable year shall, generally, be treated as a separate item of section 38 property.

4 Treas. Reg. § 1.48-12(f)(2)(i) provides:

> Solely for purposes of [former] I.R.C. § 46(c), property attributable to qualified rehabilitation expenditures will not be treated as placed in service until the building with respect to which the expenditures are made meets the definition of a qualified rehabilitated building (as defined in [former] I.R.C. § 48(g)(1) and paragraph (b) of this section) for the taxable year. Accordingly, in the first taxable year in which the building becomes a qualified rehabilitated building, the property described in [former] I.R.C. § 48(a)(1)(E) attributable to expenditures described in paragraph (c) of this section shall be considered to be placed in service, if such property was considered placed in service under [former] I.R.C. § 46(c) and the regulations thereunder without regard to this paragraph (f)(2)(i) in that taxable year or a prior taxable year.

5 *See* Section 9.2 for a description and discussion of this election.

6 Treas. Reg. § 1.46-3(d)(3).

7 Garcia v. Comm'r, 62 T.C.M. 736 (1991), T.C. Memo 1991-451.

to the master recording, the master recording was placed in service in 1983, the taxable year in which possession was transferred to the lessee.[8]

3.2 HOW DOES A TAXPAYER CLAIM THE HISTORIC TAX CREDIT?

A taxpayer claims the Historic Tax Credit by filing a Form 3468 with its tax return for the year in which the credit is claimed. The treasury regulations require that certain information be furnished with the return (either through marginal notations or a supplemented schedule), including:

(i) the beginning and ending dates of the applicable 24- or 60-month measuring period;
(ii) the adjusted basis of the building at the beginning of the measuring period; and
(iii) the amount of QREs incurred (or treated as incurred) by the taxpayer during the measuring period.[9]

If an election has been made to pass the Historic Tax Credit through to a lessee pursuant to Code § 50(d) and Treas. Reg. § 1.48-4, that fact must be reflected on the Form 3468 and a signed statement from the lessee must be included.[10] In this regard, the IRS has determined that it can require a partnership or other pass-through entity that is the lessee in such a transaction and is passing the credit through to its members to furnish the information required by Form 3468, even though it is not the owner of the qualified rehabilitated building. Similarly, the IRS may require the lessor in such a transaction to provide the lessee with the NPS project number assigned by, and the date of the final certification of completed work received from, the Secretary of the Interior in order to enable the lessee to comply with the reporting requirements of the treasury regulations.[11]

8 *See also* Feldmann v. Comm'r, 62 T.C.M. 288 (1991), T.C. Memo 1991-353; I.R.S. Priv. Ltr. Rul. 7816009 (Jan. 17, 1978).

9 Treas. Reg. § 1.48-12(b)(2)(viii). The treasury regulations also require that if, in determining compliance with the substantial rehabilitation test, the applicable adjusted basis of the building is determined in whole or in part by reference to the basis of a third party, the information furnished by the taxpayer with the Form 3468 must include a statement indicating the first day of such third party's holding period and such third party's adjusted basis at the beginning of the *later* of (i) the measuring period, or (ii) the holding period. If such information cannot be obtained by the taxpayer, the taxpayer must indicate such fact and state the manner in which adjusted basis was determined or, if different, the fair market value of the building on the applicable date.

10 Treas. Reg. § 1.48-4. *See* Section 9.2.

11 CCA 201641022.

3.3 WHAT IS A PROGRESS EXPENDITURE ELECTION?

In lieu of claiming the Historic Tax Credit commencing in the year in which the rehabilitation improvements are placed in service, Code § 47(d)(5) permits taxpayers to make a special election to claim the credit when the costs are chargeable to capital account or, when a third party contractor is involved, in the year the costs are paid. Such an election is available only in the case of "progress expenditures" incurred in connection with a rehabilitation that has a normal rehabilitation period of two years or more. Those provisions require an irrevocable election (at the partner level in the case of partnerships) that is made by filing IRS Form 3468 with the original tax return for the first taxable year to which the election applies. The progress expenditure rule provides that for "self-rehabilitated property" (i.e., property for which it is reasonable to believe more than half the QREs will be incurred directly by the taxpayer), QREs are taken into account for the taxable year in which they are properly chargeable to capital account, and for buildings that are not self-rehabilitated, QREs are taken into account when they are paid.[12] With a progress expenditure election, the credit can be taken when the expenditures are chargeable to capital account or paid, depending on whether the building is self-rehabilitated or not, regardless of when the rehabilitation improvements are placed in service.

A taxpayer may not make a progress expenditure election on an amended return that is filed after the due date for the original return (including extensions) for the tax year in question.[13]

In the case of progress expenditures incurred by a partnership, S corporation, or trust or estate, the progress expenditure election must be made separately by each partner or shareholder, or each beneficiary if the beneficiary, in determining his tax liability, would be allowed an Historic Tax Credit with respect to the expenditures. A partnership or S corporation may not make the election. A trust or estate may make the election only if, in determining its tax liability, such trust or estate would be allowed an Historic Tax Credit for the expenses that are subject to the election.[14]

In determining each partner's share of the basis attributable to QREs, the basis of the building is apportioned under the general rules relating to the allocation of QREs described in Chapter Eight.[15] If the ratio in which the "general" or "bottom line" profits of the partnership are allocated changes during the taxable year of the partnership, the ratio in effect on the date on which the progress

12 I.R.C. § 47(d)(1).

13 Treas. Reg. § 1.46-5(o)(2). Treas. Reg. §§ 1.46-1 to 1.46-6 cited herein were issued under Former Code § 46, which was repealed by Pub. L. No. 101-508, 104 Stat. 1388-1, 536–59 (1990).

14 Treas. Reg. § 1.46-5(o)(1).

15 *See* Section 8.1.

expenditures are paid or chargeable to capital account, as applicable, controls.[16] Each partner must reduce its basis for the year the building is placed in service by the amount of progress expenditures taken into account by such partner.[17]

The owner of a qualified rehabilitated building is not permitted to make an election under Former Code § 48(d) (currently Code § 50(d)(5)) to treat a lessee (or a person who will be a lessee) as having made qualified progress expenditures.[18]

It is important to note that a progress expenditure election is effective for the first taxable year for which it is made and for all subsequent taxable years unless it is revoked with the consent of the IRS. The election applies to all progress expenditures made by the taxpayer during the taxable year in connection with the rehabilitation of any "progress expenditure building." A taxpayer is not permitted to make a progress expenditure election for one building and not for others.[19] As a result of these rules, investors in syndicated Historic Tax Credit transactions rarely make the election.

3.4 CAN THE HISTORIC TAX CREDIT BE CLAIMED FOR EXPENDITURES INCURRED IN MORE THAN ONE YEAR?

If rehabilitation expenditures will be incurred over more than one year, a progress expenditure election is not made, and the 60-month phased rehabilitation rule is not applicable, it still may be possible to take credits with respect to all of the expenditures, assuming the substantial rehabilitation mathematical test can be satisfied for different 24-month periods and the building has been placed in service by the end of the first year for which credits are available. To illustrate, assume the owner of an historic building purchased the building for $100,000 on January 1, 2022 and expended $60,000 in rehabilitation expenditures during 2022, $60,000 in 2023 and $105,000 in 2024. The improvements funded with the 2022 and 2023 expenditures are placed in service on or before December 31, 2023. As of December 31, 2023, the owner's rehabilitation expenditures during the 24-month period ending on that date equal $120,000, which exceeds the owner's basis of $100,000 as of the beginning of that period, so the owner is entitled to a credit for 2023 (which will be taken ratably over years 2023 through 2027). Assume further that additional improvements are completed and placed in service in 2024. As of December 31, 2024, the owner's expenditures during the 24-month period from January 1, 2023, through December 31, 2024, equal

16 Treas. Reg. § 1.46-5(p)(2).
17 *Id.* § 1.46-5(p)(1).
18 *Id.* § 1.46-5(n).
19 *Id.* § 1.46-5(o)(1).

$165,000, which exceeds the owner's basis as of January 1, 2023, of $160,000. Therefore, the owner also would be entitled to a credit for 2024 (which will be taken ratably over years 2024 through 2028) for the rehabilitation improvements placed in service in 2024.

3.5 WHAT HAPPENS IF NPS CERTIFICATION OF THE REHABILITATION IS DELAYED?

As discussed in Chapter One, the Historic Tax Credit generally is applied ratably in equal installments over a five-year period commencing in the year in which the eligible property is placed in service. In order to qualify for the credit, however, the rehabilitation must be a certified rehabilitation of a certified historic structure.

The treasury regulations provide:

> For purposes of this section, a building shall be considered to be a certified historic structure at the time it is placed in service if the taxpayer reasonably believes on that date the building will be determined to be a certified historic structure and has requested on or before that date a determination from the Department of Interior that such building is a certified historic structure within the meaning of this paragraph (d)(1)(i) or (ii) and the Department of Interior later determines that the building is a certified historic structure.[20]

As discussed in Chapter One, compliance with a series of conditions is necessary in order for a rehabilitation to constitute a certified rehabilitation of a certified historic structure. This creates a dilemma in that the owner of a rehabilitation project may have completed the rehabilitation and placed the rehabilitation improvements in service, and thus be eligible to report the Historic Tax Credit on a tax return, prior to the receipt of final Part 3 certification from the NPS.

Fortunately, the treasury regulations provide a road map for dealing with this situation. In general, a taxpayer claiming the Historic Tax Credit must attach to the Form 3468 filed with the tax return for the taxable year in which the credit is claimed a copy of the final Part 3 certification of completed work.[21] However, the treasury regulations go on to provide:

> If the final certification of completed work has not been issued by the Secretary of the Interior at the time the tax return is filed for a year in which the credit is claimed, a copy of the first page of the Historic Preservation Certification Application—Part 2—Description of

20 *Id.* § 1.48-12(d)(1).

21 *Id.* § 1.48-12(d)(7).

> Rehabilitation (NPS Form 10-168a), with an indication that it has been received by the Department of the Interior or its designate, together with proof that the building is a certified historic structure (or that such status has been requested) must be attached to the Form 3468 filed with the return. A notice from the Department of the Interior or the State Historic Preservation Officer, stating that the nomination or application has been received, or a date-stamped nomination or application shall be sufficient indication that the nomination or application has been received. The building need not be either listed in the National Register or be determined to be of historic significance to a registered historic district at the time the return is filed for the year in which the credit is claimed. (See paragraph (d)(1) of this section.) The taxpayer must submit a copy of the final certification as an attachment to Form 3468 with the first income tax return filed after the receipt by the taxpayer of the certification. If the final certification is denied by the Department of Interior, the credit will be disallowed for any taxable year in which it was claimed. If the taxpayer fails to receive final certification of completed work prior to the date that is 30 months after the date that the taxpayer filed the tax return on which the credit was claimed, the taxpayer must submit a written statement to the District Director stating such fact prior to the last day of the 30th month, and the taxpayer shall be requested to consent to an agreement under section 6501(c)(4) extending the period of assessment for any tax relating to the time for which the credit was claimed. The procedure permitted by the preceding sentence shall be used whenever the entire rehabilitation project is not fully completed by the date that is 30 months after the taxpayer filed the tax return upon which the credit was claimed (*e.g.* a phased rehabilitation) and the Secretary of the Interior has thus not yet certified the rehabilitation.[22]

In short, as long as the taxpayer attaches a copy of a valid Part 2 approval, together with proof that an application has been made to nominate the building for a listing on the National Register or to obtain Part 1 approval that the building is of historic significance to a registered historic district, the credit may be claimed long before final Part 3 approval or the actual listing or Part 1 approval is received. However, the taxpayer is required to comply with the 30-month rule just described so as to avoid a situation in which the IRS is barred by the statute of limitations from contesting a credit because of a delay in obtaining final Part 3 approval or the actual listing of the building in the National Register or determination of significance to the registered historic district.

22 *Id.*

Interestingly, the treasury regulations do not provide that a credit will automatically be disallowed if the 30-month rule is not complied with. Instead, the IRS has concluded, based on the doctrine of equitable estoppel and other similar theories, that a taxpayer cannot assert the statute of limitations as a defense in a case where the taxpayer has not complied with the 30-month rule. The Market Segment Specialization Training Guide for the Historic Tax Credit (2002) (MSSP Training Guide) states:

> If the final certification was not obtained, and an examiner has a case either within the statute, or where the statute is barred, the taxpayer/owner should be notified, and afforded one last opportunity to obtain the proper certification from the National Park Service. If the certification is denied, and all avenues of attaining the certification have been exhausted, then the credit should be disallowed in the year taken. Lack of certification does not constitute a credit recapture under IRC section 50(a), or previously under IRC section 47(a), but in fact should be disallowed in the year taken based on the law sections which follow.
>
> Also note that the estoppel position can only be used in cases where IRS becomes aware of the lack of certification after the normal 3-year statute has expired. If you are examining a tax return that exhibits an historic credit, and you have determined that the subject building lacks the necessary certification, you should ensure that the statute is protected until the final certification is obtained, or the credit has been properly disallowed. If an examiner discovers that they have a case lacking certification where the statute is barred, and the estoppel position may be applied, they should contact their District Counsel.[23]

The treasury regulations do not specify how the 30-month rule applies in the case of a transaction involving an election under Code § 50(d)(5). Prudence would dictate having both the lessor and the lessee submit the required written statement and execute the required consent to the extension of the statute of limitations.[24]

23 MSSP Training Guide, 3-2 to 3-3, www.irs.gov/pub/irs-mssp/rehab.pdf.

24 In this regard, and although not directly on point, it is worth noting that in CCA 201641022, the IRS Chief Counsel's Office concluded that the IRS can require the lessee in an historic master lease transaction involving a pass-through of the Historic Tax Credit under Code § 50(d)(5) and Treas. Reg. § 1.48-4 to file a Form 3468 providing information necessary to enable the IRS to trace the credit from the credit claimant to the entity that incurs the QREs. See Section 3.2.

Chapter Four

Availability of the Historic Tax Credit to Transferees

The Code provides that the cost of acquiring a building or an interest therein is specifically excluded from the definition of a QRE.[1] However, where QREs are incurred by an owner of property, and a taxpayer acquires the property attributable to such expenditures (or an interest therein) before such property is placed in service, the taxpayer is treated as having incurred the expenditures at the time that they were incurred by the prior owner, subject to certain limitations (and, therefore, is entitled to the Historic Tax Credit with respect to such expenditures). In particular, the regulations state:

> (3) *Incurred by the taxpayer*—(i) *In general.* Qualified rehabilitation expenditures are incurred by the taxpayer for purposes of this section on the date such expenditures would be considered incurred under an accrual method of accounting, regardless of the method of accounting used by the taxpayer with respect to other items of income and expense. If qualified rehabilitation expenditures are treated as having been incurred by a taxpayer under paragraph (c)(3)(ii) of this section, the taxpayer shall be treated as having incurred the expenditures on the date such expenditures were incurred by the transferor.
>
> (ii) Qualified rehabilitation expenditures treated as incurred by the taxpayer—
>
> (A) Where rehabilitation expenditures are incurred with respect to a building by a person (or persons) other than the taxpayer and the taxpayer subsequently acquires the building, or a portion of the building to which some or all of the expenditures are allocable (e.g., a condominium unit to which rehabilitation expenditures have been allocated), the taxpayer acquiring such property shall be treated as having incurred the rehabilitation expenditures actually incurred by the transferor (or treated as incurred by the transferor under this paragraph (c)(3)(ii)) allocable to the acquired property, provided that—

1 I.R.C. § 47(c)(2)(B)(ii).

(*1*) The building, or the portion of the building, acquired by the taxpayer was not used (or, if later, was not placed in service (as defined in paragraph (f)(2) of this section)) after the rehabilitation expenditures were incurred and prior to the date of acquisition, and

(*2*) No credit with respect to such qualified rehabilitation expenditures is claimed by anyone other than the taxpayer acquiring the property. For purposes of this paragraph (c)(3)(ii), use shall mean actual use, whether personal or business. In the case of a building that is divided into condominium units, expenditures attributable to the common elements shall be allocable to the individual condominium units in accordance with the principles of paragraph (c)(10)(ii) of this section. Furthermore, for purpose of this paragraph (c)(3)(ii), a condominium unit's share of the common elements shall not be considered to have been used (or placed in service) prior to the time that the particular condominium unit is used.

(B) The amount of rehabilitation expenditures described in paragraph (c)(3)(ii)(A) of this section treated as incurred by the taxpayer under this paragraph shall be the lesser of—

(*1*) The amount of rehabilitation expenditures incurred before the date on which the taxpayer acquired the building (or portion thereof) to which the rehabilitation expenditures are attributable, or

(*2*) The portion of the taxpayer's cost or other basis for the property that is properly allocable to the property resulting from the rehabilitation expenditures described in paragraph (c)(3)(ii)(B)(1) of this section.

(C) For purposes of this paragraph (c)(3)(ii), the amount of rehabilitation expenditures treated as incurred by the taxpayer under this paragraph (c) shall not be treated as costs for the acquisition of a building. The portion of the cost of acquiring a building (or an interest therein) that is not treated under this paragraph as qualified rehabilitation expenditures incurred by the taxpayer is not treated as section 38 property in the hands of the acquiring taxpayer. (*See* paragraph (c)(7)(ii) of this section.) (*See* paragraph (b)(2)(vii) for rules concerning the application of the substantial rehabilitation test when expenditures are treated as incurred by the taxpayer.)[2]

Under these provisions of the treasury regulations, the transferee is treated as having incurred the expenditures that were incurred by the transferor on the date that the transferor incurred the expenditures.[3] For purposes of applying the substantial rehabilitation test described in Chapter Two, the transferee's

2 Treas. Reg. § 1.48-12(c)(3).

3 *Id.* § 1.48-12(c)(3)(i).

adjusted basis in the building is determined as of the beginning of the first day of the 24-month (or 60-month) measuring period, or, if later, the first day of the transferee's holding period.[4] However, if the later date is used, the transferee's basis as of the first day of the transferee's holding period is considered to be equal to the transferee's basis in the building on that date *minus* (i) the amount of any QREs treated as having been incurred by the transferee, and (ii) the amount of QREs incurred before the transfer and during the 24-month period by any other person having an interest in the building (e.g., a person to whom the transferor leased space in the building). The treasury regulations go on to provide that this special rule for computing the basis of the transferee as of the first day of the transferee's holding period does not apply unless the transferee's basis in the building is determined with reference to (i) the transferee's cost of the building (including rehabilitation expenditures), (ii) the transferor's basis in the building (where such basis includes the amount of the expenditures), or (iii) any other amount that includes the cost of the rehabilitation expenditures.[5]

The IRS has issued several private letter rulings illustrating the application of the transferee rules in the context of rehabilitations involving condominium units.[6]

4 *Id.* § 1.48-12(b)(2)(vii).

5 *Id.*

6 *See, e.g.*, Priv. Ltr. Ruls. 8243168 (July 28, 1982), 8333026 (May 13, 1983), 8639026 (June 26, 1986).

Chapter Five

Special Issues in Multi-Owner and Multiple-Building Historic Tax Credit Projects

5.1 CONDOMINIUMS

It is not uncommon for a qualified rehabilitated building to be owned in condominium fashion. In order to qualify for the Historic Tax Credit, a condominium unit must be used in a trade or business or for the production of income. Accordingly, an owner-occupied residential unit will not be eligible. However, both residential rental and commercial properties do qualify. In this regard, it is important to remember that, while a condominium unit may be treated as a "building" for purposes of the low-income housing tax credit described in Code § 42, that is not the case for the Historic Tax Credit. It is the physical structure rather than the form of ownership that constitutes a "building" for Historic Tax Credit purposes.[1]

For purposes of determining the adjusted basis of a building in applying the substantial rehabilitation test described in Chapter Two, if the building is divided into condominium units, the term "adjusted basis" means the aggregate adjusted basis of all the respective condominium owners.[2] Similarly, for purposes of determining the aggregate QREs incurred during the applicable measuring period, a condominium unit owner may include the expenditures incurred by the other condominium owners.[3] Moreover, in determining the amount of QREs treated as incurred by a taxpayer who acquires a building or a portion of the building subsequent to the time the expenses were incurred, the regulations specifically make reference to "a condominium unit to which rehabilitation expenditures have been allocated."[4] The same section of the regulations provides that, for purposes of applying the special transferee rule, in the case of a building that is divided into condominium units, expenditures attributable to the common elements are allocable to the individual condominium units in accordance with the principles set forth in Treas. Reg. § 1.48-12(c)(10)(ii)

1 See Section 1.2.2.
2 Treas. Reg. § 1.48-12(b)(2(iii)(B).
3 *Id.* § 1.48-12(b)(2)(vi).
4 *Id.* § 1.48-12(b)(3)(ii).

and that, for purposes of the prior use or placement in service test in Treas. Reg. § 1.48-12(c)(3)(ii), a condominium unit's share of the common elements shall not be considered to have been used (or placed in service) prior to the time that the particular condominium unit is used.[5]

Note that, in the case of a qualified rehabilitated building owned in condominium fashion, the NPS normally will require, as part of the historic certification process, evidence that the bylaws or other governing documents of the condominium protect the building from alterations or changes that fail to meet the Standards of Rehabilitation.

5.2 FUNCTIONALLY RELATED BUILDINGS: AN OVERVIEW

Many larger historic rehabilitation projects involve multiple buildings located in a mill complex, former military base, college campus, or similar area. In such cases, multiple ownership issues become substantially more complicated. NPS regulations generally state that properties containing more than one building where the buildings are determined by the NPS to have been "functionally related to serve an overall purpose" will be treated as a single certified historic structure.[6] This raises a number of potential problems. In the first place, even if all of the rehabilitation work is performed by the same developer (or a related entity), work on one building easily could affect the historic character of other buildings within the group. Moreover, the aggregation of all buildings in a large project as a single historic structure creates delays in obtaining Part 3 approval for the earlier rehabilitation work.

The potential problems proliferate when the buildings are owned by separate developers, particularly when the developers have different goals. For example, some may want to demolish or sell off buildings, while others intend to undertake substantial rehabilitation projects. In such a situation, the actions of other owners may affect the eligibility of the rehabilitated buildings for the Historic Tax Credit. While the owner of a building or buildings for which historic certification is being requested normally is responsible only for the work it undertakes on its own property, the NPS looks askance at efforts to artificially separate ownership in a functionally related complex. In addition, if other owners redevelop, alter, demolish, or otherwise dispose of functionally related buildings that cause the overall complex to lose its historic integrity, Historic Tax Credits may not be available to the owner requesting certification.

5.2.1 Functionally Related Buildings: NPS Guidance

Additional guidance relating to functionally related buildings is available on the NPS website and is summarized as follows.

5 *Id.* § 1.48-12(c)(3)(ii).

6 36 C.F.R. § 67.4(e).

As noted earlier, under NPS regulations, historic buildings that are determined to be "functionally related historically" are treated as a "single certified historic structure" for the purposes of certification when rehabilitated as part of an overall project. The regulations provide that certification of a completed rehabilitation for such a group of buildings is "issued on the merits of the overall project rather than for each structure or individual component."[7]

Under such additional guidance, the determination of whether a project includes buildings functionally related historically is made by the NPS on a case-by-case basis, taking into account all of the relevant facts and circumstances. The guidance sets forth the criteria to be used by the NPS to make such determinations as well as a lengthy list of property types and examples—such as a mill complex, a campus of institutional buildings, a military base, a public housing complex, a farm, or a residence with a carriage house.

Consistent with NPS regulations, buildings that are functionally related historically are treated as one project for the purposes of certification. It is important to note that buildings owned by different legal entities may still be considered part of one overall rehabilitation project depending on their beneficial ownership and control, as well as other facts and circumstances. In most cases, buildings owned by unrelated parties will be treated as separate projects.

The NPS believes certification should be based on the "cumulative effect" of the overall project, rather than on each individual building. When applied to multiple-building projects, the "cumulative effect" standard provides added flexibility to the NPS in reviewing projects, including the allowance of some demolition in limited circumstances, as identified in the regulations.[8] In such cases, work on an individual building that does not meet the Secretary of the Interior's Standards for Rehabilitation, and would otherwise cause that individual building rehabilitation not to be certified, may still be certified for Historic Tax Credit purposes as part of an overall project that meets the Standards.

In general, the rehabilitation of buildings that are functionally related historically and owned by the same or related parties is treated as one project for the purposes of certification, and such buildings are certified by the NPS as one project after the rehabilitation of the final building in the project is completed. However, in certain limited circumstances described herein, the NPS has identified situations in which the rehabilitation of such buildings may be treated as separate projects for the purposes of certification.

A determination by the NPS that the rehabilitation of functionally related buildings may be treated as separate projects generally is made at the beginning of the overall project and is based on facts and circumstances relating to the overall project and on the examples provided in the NPS guidance. Such

7 36 C.F.R. §§ 67.4(e), 67.6(b)(4)–(5).

8 *Id.* § 67.6(b)(5).

guidance also assumes that an entire property owned by the same or related parties will be rehabilitated as a certified rehabilitation project or projects and that the effect on the property's overall historic character will be no different whether rehabilitated as one or more separate projects.

When projects are considered to be separate, the certification of each project will be issued independently of any other project, with each project required to meet the Standards on its own merits in order to be certified. Any other work undertaken on the overall property within five years following the completion of any individual rehabilitation project, even if such work is part of a separate rehabilitation project, will still need to be submitted for review by the NPS and could affect the certification of other prior, current, or planned projects. As is the case with any rehabilitation project, a certification may be revoked within five years following completion of the rehabilitation in the case of work not undertaken as represented by the owner in the Part 3 application or work undertaken after certification that is inconsistent with the Standards.[9] In addition, a property that is determined to have lost the qualities required for individual listing on the National Register may be de-listed, and a building that is determined to no longer possess the qualities to be designated as a certified historic structure may be certified as non-contributing.[10]

Owners of buildings that are functionally related historically must include with their Part 1 applications a site plan showing all the buildings and ownership information for the entire historic property, whether or not all of the buildings comprising such property are owned by the same or related parties. For buildings owned by the same or related parties, the applications also must include exterior and interior photographs of the buildings (whether or not work is proposed to the individual building), the timing of the work for each building (i.e., the estimated start and completion dates), and such other information and materials identifying the facts and circumstances (e.g., the construction dates and historic uses of the individual buildings) as the NPS may require under its guidance.

The NPS strongly recommends that projects containing functionally related buildings be discussed with the SHPO on a preliminary consultation basis prior to submitting a Part 1 application so that the SHPO can advise the owner and discuss the project with the NPS if necessary.

In the case of projects covered by the NPS guidance, the owner must elect whether to submit the proposed rehabilitation as one or multiple projects at the start of the rehabilitation. Such guidance cannot be applied retroactively. In other words, an owner cannot assume that the proposed rehabilitation of a multiple-building complex will be treated as separate projects for the purpose

9 *Id.* § 67.6(e).

10 *Id.* § 66.6(f).

of certification based solely on the NPS's published guidance. A final determination as to the proper characterization of each project will be based on the specific facts and circumstances of such project and will be determined by the NPS solely based on its review of the project's Part 1 and 2 applications.

The NPS guidance contains a number of detailed examples, a discussion of which is beyond the scope of this book. Such examples are meant to be read and applied in toto, as the applicability of one or more examples to the facts and circumstances of any individual project will vary. Some of the examples are dependent on meeting a planned minimum "gap" period between separate projects during which no rehabilitation work is occurring on the property. It is the owner's responsibility to ensure that each project's scope and timing are undertaken consistent with the guidance and the Part 1 and 2 applications as approved; otherwise, the guidance may not apply to the project, including whether a project continues to qualify as a separate project for the purposes of certification. Separate rehabilitation projects must meet the Standards on their own merit and cannot take into account the cumulative effect of prior or other work undertaken as separate certified projects. When unforeseen circumstances arise involving a project (such as unanticipated market or financing conditions illustrated in the examples contained in the guidance) that has already received a Part 2 decision by the NPS, any request to change the scope of the project should be made in an amendment to the Part 2 application.

The examples in the guidance address a wide variety of fact patterns. For example, functionally related buildings with the same or related owners rehabilitated as part of a larger overall project may be treated as separate projects for the purposes of certification when there is a substantial break in rehabilitation activity—that is, a minimum period of one year during which no rehabilitation work is occurring on the property.

NPS guidance also provides examples addressing large functionally related complexes where certain structures, sites, and environments functioned in effect as separate properties; and for which structures, sites, and environments are considered to have been "functionally related historically" in a geographically distinct usage-related grouping.

While the number of buildings alone is not the sole determinant for the NPS guidance to be applicable, functionally related complexes typically have a large number of buildings that serve different and diverse uses (i.e., a large *and* diverse property) for the examples to be applicable. Under the applicable guidance, in order to be treated as a separate project for the purposes of certification, a specified group of buildings must have functioned together historically as a geographically discrete, related grouping. Under this approach, a mill typically would not be considered to be a large and diverse property by itself, whereas a mill complex with separate housing for workers might be so treated. Military bases and medical, university, corporate, and other institutional campuses are examples of properties that typically would be subject to NPS guidance on very large and diverse properties.

In most cases, individual projects that are part of a large and diverse historic property will be certified separately and independently from one another. Work undertaken in connection with one project that does not satisfy the Standards generally will not impact the certification of another project. However, if such work has an adverse impact on the qualities that caused the property to be nominated for listing in the National Register or on the setting and environment of the individual buildings in another project, it could impact the certification of other projects and/or the status of the individual buildings in such projects as certified historic structures if the work occurs within five years following the completion of any approved projects.[11]

The guidance contains other examples of projects involving functionally related buildings that may be treated as separate projects for the purposes of certification based on the following facts and circumstances, dependent upon a series of factors identified in the guidance, including:

(i) A functionally related complex where at the beginning of the project the owner plans to own and rehabilitate only part of the complex, begins work, and later, after substantially completing or when nearing completion of the project, acquires one or more additional buildings in the complex that were not previously planned or anticipated to be part of the original project.

(ii) Large, functionally related complexes under common ownership and in continuous historic use (such as large factories, institutional campuses, and resort properties for which continued operation often depends on an ongoing, continual rehabilitation of the property). In such cases where the ongoing work involves the substantial rehabilitation of individual buildings or groups of buildings that are part of a large and diverse property, the NPS will take into account the specific facts and circumstances that relate to the needs of such a continuously operating property in determining whether to treat such work as a separate project for the purposes of certification. These factors include, but are not limited to, the scheduling of the rehabilitation work on individual buildings; the proximity, design, and function of the individual buildings; and the historic evolution of the property.

(iii) Functionally related complexes under common ownership where the rehabilitation involves multiple buildings and will extend well beyond a 60-month phased-project time period.

(iv) Large housing complexes consisting of many separate or semi-attached houses or buildings, multiple streets, and shared land area under common ownership.

(v) Functionally related complexes where all the buildings were originally planned to be rehabilitated, but later, because of financing or other reasons, work was never initiated for some of the buildings, and future plans for the buildings are uncertain.

(vi) Functionally related complexes where the proposed rehabilitation cannot be treated as separate projects and still meet the Standards.

11 *Id.* § 67.6(f).

Chapter Six

Qualified Rehabilitation Expenditures

Only QREs are eligible for the Historic Tax Credit. A QRE includes any amount chargeable to capital account and incurred in connection with the rehabilitation (including reconstruction) of a "qualified rehabilitated building" that is depreciable under Code § 168 and that is (i) nonresidential real property, (ii) residential rental property, or (iii) real property having a class life of more than 12.5 years.[1] A qualified rehabilitated building means a building (and its structural components) if (i) such building has been substantially rehabilitated, (ii) such building was placed in service before the beginning of the rehabilitation, (iii) such building is a certified historic structure, and (iv) depreciation (or amortization in lieu of depreciation) is allowable with respect to the building.[2] As noted earlier, the Code provides that the Historic Tax Credit is not available in the case of the rehabilitation of property used predominantly to furnish lodging unless the property is a certified historic structure.[3] Under current law, this provision is somewhat meaningless since *any* qualified rehabilitated building must be a certified historic structure.[4]

The treasury regulations provide that an expenditure will be deemed to be incurred on the date it would be considered to be incurred under the accrual method of accounting even if the taxpayer is not using the accrual method for other purposes.[5]

The regulations generally define a building to mean any structure or edifice enclosing a space within its walls, and usually covered by a roof, the purposes of which is, for example, to provide shelter or housing, or to provide working, office, parking, display, or sales space.[6]

---

1 I.R.C. § 47(c)(2).

2 *Id.* § 47(c)(1).

3 *Id.* § 50(b)(2).

4 *Id.* § 47(c)(1)(A)(iii).

5 Treas. Reg. § 1.48-12(c)(3)(i).

6 *Id.* § 1.48-1(e)(1). The IRS also has indicated that a sports stadium can be considered to be a building. *See* Rehabilitation Credit (Historic Preservation) FAQs, citing Treas. Reg. § 1.48-1(e) and Rev. Rul. 69-170, 1969-1 CB 28.

The costs of the structural components of a building may be QREs if the amounts are properly included in the basis of depreciable property that is nonresidential real property, residential rental property, real property that has a class life of more than 12.5 years, or an addition or improvement to the preceding three types of property. The regulations include the following list of examples of structural components.[7]

- Walls
- Partitions
- Floors
- Ceilings
- Permanent coverings of walls, partitions, floors and ceilings, such as paneling or tiles
- Windows and doors
- Components of central air-conditioning or heating systems
- Plumbing and plumbing fixtures
- Electrical wiring and lighting fixtures
- Chimneys
- Stairs
- Escalators
- Elevators
- Sprinkler systems
- Fire escapes
- Other components (that is, other parts of the building) relating to the operation or maintenance of the building)

The treasury regulations state that QREs include costs incurred for architectural and engineering fees, site survey fees, legal expenses, insurance premiums, development fees, construction management fees, and other construction-related costs to the extent that they are properly added to the basis of the real property.[8] The IRS also has ruled that the capitalized expenses of cleaning up fire damage to a qualified building will be treated as QREs.[9]

Although not specifically listed in the treasury regulations, the IRS has issued guidance stating that the following costs may be QREs if the amounts are properly included in the basis of depreciable property that is nonresidential real property, residential rental property, real property that has a class life of more than 12.5 years, or an addition or improvement to the preceding three types of property.[10]

7 *Id.* § 1.48-1(e)(2).

8 *Id.* § 1.48-12(c)(2).

9 Priv. Ltr. Rul. 9145019 (Aug. 6, 1991).

10 Rehabilitation Tax Credit—Real Estate Tax Tips, IRS, Apr. 22, 2022, www.irs.gov/pub/irs-utl/qualified-rehabilitation-expenditures.pdf.

- Permanently installed operable floodgates
- Permanently attached fastening devices to hold floodgates or to attach flood wrapping systems
- A retaining wall that is part of or connected to the structure of the building
- A seawall that is part of or connected to the structure of the building
- The portion of landscaping designed only to protect the building (e.g., drains and regrading for drainage)
- Elevated structure built to protect utilities (such as a freestanding air-conditioning unit on a raised platform adjacent the building)
- Structural reinforcing and improvements to foundation (to withstand hydrostatic and hydrodynamic pressure)
- Applying waterproof coating to the exterior of the foundation walls, whether above or below grade
- Costs associated with excavation and/or sitework necessary to access an exterior foundation or basement walls in order to undertake structural improvements or to apply waterproof coatings
- Permanently installed vents or drains (inside or outside)
- Sump pumps (only if permanently installed and/or if connected to drainage system)
- Materials to fill in the basement (sand, gravel, etc.) and the installation/compacting of the material
- Basement drains
- Moving utilities inside the building
- In a documented floodplain, lifting/elevating at the same site (lifting the building onto a new, taller foundation) with no additional square footage underneath the building (open space (such as a building on posts pilings) or crawl space below)
- Lifting/elevating a building on an enclosed foundation with occupiable space below the first floor that is used for parking, storage, or other limited uses allowed by a flood ordinance
- New foundation construction including break-away walls, louvers, lattice, or other architectural screenings
- Where a current site is threatened or destroyed, moving the historic building including:
  - Lifting the building on the original site and transporting it to the new site
  - New site preparation
  - New foundation
  - Permits for and relating to the move (e.g., utility fees for moving traffic light out of the way, etc.)
  - Utility connections at the new location

The IRS has made it clear in the MSSP Training Guide that development fees will be carefully scrutinized to determine whether they are properly characterized as QREs or should be recharacterized as syndication costs, organization costs, acquisition costs, rent up/lease costs, or management fees.[11]

QREs do *not* include:

(i) any expenditure for which the straight-line MACRS depreciation method or the straight-line depreciation method under the "alternative depreciation system" is not used;
(ii) the cost of acquiring any building or interest therein;
(iii) the cost of enlarging an existing building;
(iv) the rehabilitation of a certified historic structure that is not certified in accordance with the provisions of Code § 47(c)(2)(C);
(v) expenditures incurred in connection with the rehabilitation of a building which is allocable to the portion of such property which is (or may reasonably be expected to be) tax-exempt use property (within the meaning of Code § 168(h), except that "50 percent" shall be substituted for "35 percent" in Code § 168(h)(1)(B)(iii)); or
(vi) expenditures incurred by a lessee of a building if, on the date on which the rehabilitation is completed, the remaining term of the lease (without regard to renewal periods) is less than the statutory recovery period for the building set forth in Code § 168(c).[12]

In published guidance by the IRS, only those amounts that are capitalized in connection with the rehabilitation of structural and architectural features of a building that is a certified historic structure will qualify as QREs, with the guidance stating that the following costs associated with such items generally are not eligible.[13]

- Acquisition costs
- Appliances not either real or residential rental property
- Office equipment
- Cabinets (unless an inherently permanent structure and part of the building)
- Carpeting (if tacked in place and not glued)—Rev. Rul. 67-349; *Hospital Corp. of America v. Commissioner*, 109 T.C. 21 (1997)
- Decks, porches, and porticos (that were not part of original building)
- Demolition and removal costs (of an existing building on property site)

11 MSSP Training Guide, 19-1 to 19-6 (2002).

12 I.R.C. § 47(c)(2)(B). *See also* Au v. Comm'r, 59 T.C.M. 458 (1990), T.C. Memo 1990-203; Girgis v. Comm'r, 61 T.C.M. 2516 (1991), T.C. Memo 1991-191; S. Rep. No. 97-144 (Pub. L. No. 97-34), at 73; H.R. Rep. No. 95-600, at 88 (1978); S. Rep. No. 99-313 (Pub. L. No. 99-510), at 7514.

13 Rehabilitation Tax Credit, *supra* note 10.

- Fencing
- Feasibility studies
- Financing fees (such as mortgage-related financing not during the construction period)
- Furniture
- Landscaping
- Leasing expenses
- New construction costs or enlargement costs (increase in total volume from original building)
- Outdoor lighting (remote from building)
- Parking lot
- Paving
- Planters/pots
- Retaining walls that are not part of a building and its structural components
- Sidewalks
- Signage
- Storm sewer construction costs
- Window treatments
- Display racks and shelves
- Production machinery
- Grocery counters
- Temporary protective measure like sandbags, inflatable dams, etc.
- Levy
- Retaining wall that is not part of or connected to the structure of the building
- Temporary floodgates/flood shields
- Lifting/elevating a building on an enclosed foundation with occupiable space below the first floor that is used as additional living areas (expansion of the building)
- Attachments for pulley or other system to relocate furnishings above flood level

Solar panels, wind turbines, and geothermal systems generally are five-year property under Code § 168.[14] The costs of solar panels, wind turbines, and geothermal systems described in Code § 168(e)(3)(B)(vi)(1) are not included in the basis of the building and, therefore, should not qualify for the Historic Tax Credit. Additionally, under Code § 48(a)(2)(B), the same property that is used to claim an Historic Tax Credit cannot also be used to claim an energy credit.

14 *See* I.R.C. § 168(e)(3)(B)(vi)(1).

As indicated earlier, the Code provides that any expenditures attributable to the enlargement of a building are excluded from the definition of QREs.[15] The treasury regulations go on to provide that a building will be deemed to be enlarged to the extent that the total volume of the building is increased.[16] The total volume of a building is determined by multiplying (i) the floor area of the base of the building by (ii) the height from the underside of the lowest floor (including the basement) to the average height of the furnished roof (as it exists or existed). Floor area is measured from the exterior faces of external walls (other than shared walls) and from the centerline of shared walls that are external walls.[17] An increase in floor space that results from interior remodeling will not be considered to be an enlargement.[18]

Expenditures that are only partially attributable to the enlargement of a building must be allocated between the building and the enlargement. If the taxpayer is unable to document a specific allocation of the expenditures, the allocation must be made on some other reasonable basis such as the type of improvement and how the improvement relates functionally to the building. For example, the treasury regulations provide that in the case of expenditures for a roof or an air-conditioning system, it would be reasonable for the taxpayer to allocate such expenditures between the two portions based on the volume of the building, excluding the enlargement, served by the roof or the air-conditioning system relative to the volume of the enlargement served by the improvement.[19]

The IRS takes the position that demolition costs that result in the complete removal or elimination of a building will not qualify for the Historic Tax Credit. On the other hand, if the building continues to exist after the demolition costs are incurred, the IRS apparently will permit the inclusion of such costs as QREs. The IRS has conceded that most rehabilitations involve some "light interior demolition" that typically consists of interior work to reconfigure areas or to clean out an older abandoned building.

15 I.R.C. § 47(c)(2)(B)(iii).

16 Treas. Reg. § 1.48-12(c)(10)(i).

17 *Id.*

18 *Id. See also* Priv. Ltr. Rul. 200518016 (May 6, 2005), in which the IRS ruled that the cost of replacing the outside wooden stairs of an historic building did not qualify for the credit because such stairs would increase the total volume of the building.

19 Treas. Reg. § 1.48-12(c)(10)(ii).

Chapter Seven

Limitations on the Use of the Historic Tax Credit for Property Used by Exempt Organizations or Governmental Units or Foreign Persons or Entities

7.1 OVERVIEW

The Code generally provides that no investment tax credit is available with respect to property "used by" a tax-exempt organization (other than a cooperative described in Code § 521) "unless such property is used predominantly in an unrelated trade or business the income of which is subject to tax under section 511."[1] However, if a qualified rehabilitated building is used by a tax-exempt organization *pursuant to a lease*, such limitation will not apply.[2] Similarly, in general, no credit is available with respect to

> any property used (i) by the United States, any State or political subdivision thereof, any possession of the United States, or any agency or instrumentality of any of the foregoing, or (ii) by any foreign person or entity (as defined in Code § 168(h)(2)(C)), but only with respect to property to which Code § 168(h)(2)(A)(iii) applies (determined after the application of Code § 168(h)(2)(B)).[3]

However, an exception to this rule applies to any "qualified rehabilitated building *leased to* a governmental unit (or a foreign person or entity)."[4] It is not clear whether the words "pursuant to a lease" in Code § 50(b)(3) were intended to have a different substantive effect than the words "leased to" in Code § 50(b)(4). Read literally, the Code § 50(b)(4) exception is narrower in scope.

Neither Code § 50(b)(3) nor Code § 50(b)(4) applies to any property "by reason of use under a lease with a term of less than 6 months (determined under Code § 168(i)(3))."[5] Moreover, in applying these provisions to property owned by or leased to partnerships, "rules similar to the rules of paragraphs (5) and

1 I.R.C. § 50(b)(3).
2 *Id.* (emphasis added).
3 *Id.* § 50(b)(4).
4 *Id.* § 50(b)(4)(C) (emphasis added).
5 *Id.* § 50(b)(4)(B).

(6) of Code § 168(h) shall apply."[6] Finally, the provisions of Code §§ 50(b)(3) and 50(b)(4) generally are subject to the special rules set forth in Code § 168(h). These rules are discussed in Section 7.2.

Notwithstanding the language of Former Code § 48(a)(5) (currently Code § 50(b)(4)), in a private letter ruling issued in 1986, the IRS ruled that where property was owned by a municipality and leased to a limited partnership for a term in excess of 19 years, lessee improvements with a useful life of 19 years that otherwise qualified for the Historic Tax Credit would not be disqualified by the provisions of Code § 50(b)(4) (Former Code § 48(a)(5)), since the unexpired term of the lease would exceed the useful life of the rehabilitation improvements. As a result, the municipality would not be deemed to acquire the improvements upon the termination of the lease.[7]

It is useful to review the facts of this ruling. In the ruling, a limited partnership with a corporate general partner and two unrelated corporations as limited partners was formed to rehabilitate a project in a city. The city acquired the project property from the United States under the Federal Property and Administrative Services Act of 1940. The consideration for the acquisition was stated to be the perpetual use and maintenance of the property as and for an historic monument. The property was leased by the city to the limited partnership, which then rehabilitated the property into a facility to provide transient lodging, restaurant facilities, and customary amenities of a hotel.

The lease terms implied (but apparently did not explicitly state) that title to the tenant improvements would reside in the partnership during the term of the lease. The partnership would operate the hotel and lease the restaurant facility to an unrelated entity that would operate the restaurant. The renovation was financed through a combination of the syndication of limited partnership interests in the partnership and industrial development bond financing. In addition, the partnership borrowed certain amounts from the city, which the city obtained in part through an urban development action grant.

The project was listed in the National Register of Historic Places, and the rehabilitation was certified by the Secretary of the Interior as being consistent with the historic character of the project.

---

6 *Id.* § 50(b)(4)(D). Paragraph (5) of I.R.C. § 168(h) provides in part that "the determination of whether any portion of [property leased to a partnership] is tax-exempt use property shall be made by treating each tax-exempt entity partner's proportionate share . . . of such property as being leased to such partner." Paragraph (6) of I.R.C. § 168(h) provides that certain property may be deemed to be tax-exempt use property if any allocation to a tax-exempt entity under a partnership agreement is not a "qualified allocation."

7 Priv. Ltr. Rul. 8641024 (July 10, 1986).

The IRS ruled that the rehabilitation expenditures to be incurred by the limited partnership would be QREs and that the portion of the basis of the project attributable to those expenditures constituted "new section 38 property" under Former Code § 48(a)(1)(E). The IRS also ruled that the portion of the basis of the project that was attributable to QREs would not be deemed to be "used by" a governmental unit under Former Code § 48(a)(5) (currently Code § 50(b)(4)).

In the ruling, the IRS concluded that the project would not be "used by" a governmental unit within the meaning of Former Code § 48(a)(5) despite the fact that the term "used by" includes ownership by a government unit even if leased to another person under the treasury regulations.[8] In the case of a qualified rehabilitated building, the IRS pointed out that the term "section 38 property" means the portion of the basis that is attributable to QREs, citing Former Code § 48(a)(1)(E). The taxpayer in the ruling represented that the partnership would incur the QREs. In addition, the IRS focused on the fact that the term of the lease (including its renewal options) would be substantially in excess of the anticipated useful life of the rehabilitation improvements. As a result, the city would not acquire the rehabilitation improvements upon the termination of the lease. The IRS concluded that the section 38 property consisting of the portion of the basis of the property attributable to QREs would not be owned or "used by" the city and that Former Code § 48(a)(5) would not apply.

The IRS observed that the legislative history of the Tax Reform Act of 1984 reflected the intent of Congress that improvements constructed by taxable lessees qualify for the investment tax credit notwithstanding the tax-exempt status of the lessor. The committee reports at the time of such tax legislation stated that: "[t]ax-exempt use property does not include improvements constructed by a taxable entity on underlying land or other property leased from a tax-exempt entity merely because the tax-exempt entity is the owner of the land or other property."[9]

It is important to note that a private letter ruling is directed only to the taxpayer who requested it and may not be used or cited as precedent by other taxpayers.[10] However, the rationale expressed in the ruling is rooted in logic and appears to represent a reasonable interpretation of the provisions of Code § 50(b)(4) in the context of the legislative history and intent of such provisions. Taxpayers who intend to rely on the rationale of this ruling should attempt to structure their transaction in a manner that matches the fact situation described in the ruling to the greatest extent possible.

8 Treas. Reg. § 1.48-1(k).

9 H.R. Rep. No. 98-432, pt. 2, at 1147 (1984); S. Comm. on Fin., 98th Cong., Explanation of Provisions Approved by the Comm. on Mar. 21, 1984 (Comm. Print 1984).

10 I.R.C. § 6110(k)(3).

7.2 HOW DO THE TAX-EXEMPT USE PROPERTY RULES AFFECT THE ABILITY OF A TAXPAYER TO CLAIM THE HISTORIC TAX CREDIT?

7.2.1 Overview

Code § 168(h) contains a comprehensive set of rules dealing with leases of property to "tax-exempt entities." Under these rules, real property that is leased to a tax-exempt entity in a "disqualified lease" is treated as "tax-exempt use property." Tax-exempt use real property must be depreciated using the straight-line method (without regard to salvage value) over the longer of (i) 30 years (in the case of residential rental property) or 40 years (in the case of nonresidential real property), or (ii) 125 percent of the lease term. In addition, expenses that otherwise would constitute QREs eligible for the Historic Tax Credit are ineligible for such credit.

The Code provides that the term "tax-exempt use property" does not include "any portion of a property if such portion is predominantly used by the tax-exempt entity (directly or through a partnership of which such entity is a partner) in an unrelated trade or business the income of which is subject to tax under Code § 511."[11] The legislative history of the provision provides that property will not be treated as predominantly used by the tax-exempt entity in an unrelated trade or business, the income of which is subject to tax under Code § 511, merely because the property is debt-financed property under Code § 514.[12] The same rule applies in the context of property owned by a partnership that has both a tax-exempt entity (or tax-exempt controlled entity) and a person who is not a tax-exempt entity as partners.

For purposes of applying the foregoing rules, the term "tax-exempt entity" includes governmental entities and tax-exempt organizations, as well as foreign persons and entities. Moreover, "any organization which is engaged in activities substantially similar to those engaged in by a predecessor organization shall succeed to the treatment under this subparagraph of such predecessor organization."[13] Property is treated as first being used by an organization "when the property is first placed in service under a lease to such organization, or in the case of property leased to (or held by) a partnership (or other pass-thru entity) in which the organization is a member, the later of when such property is first used by such partnership or pass-thru entity or when such organization is first a member of such partnership or pass-thru entity."[14]

A disqualified lease is defined as:

> any lease of the property to a tax-exempt entity but only if—(I) part or all of the property was financed (directly or indirectly) by an obligation,

11 *Id.* § 168(h)(1)(D).

12 H.R. Rep. No. 98-861, at 791 (1984) (Conf. Rep.), 1984-3 C.B. (Vol. 2) 45.

13 I.R.C. § 168(h)(2)(E)(iii).

14 *Id.* § 168(h)(2)(E)(iv).

> the interest on which is exempt from tax under Code § 103(a) and such entity (or a related entity) participated in such financing; (II) under such lease there is a fixed or determinable price purchase or sale option which involves such entity (or a related entity) or there is the equivalent of such an option; (III) such lease has a lease term in excess of 20 years; or (IV) such lease occurs after a sale (or other transfer) of the property by, or lease of the property from, such entity (or a related entity) and such property has been used by such entity (or a related entity) before such sale (or other transfer) or lease.[15]

If only part of a building is leased to a tax-exempt entity in a disqualified lease, the taxpayer must determine the amount of the building's unadjusted basis that is allocable to the portion of the building that is tax-exempt use property. This computation is based on the percentage that the square footage of the building that is tax-exempt use property (excluding common areas) bears to the total square footage in the building (excluding common areas).[16]

It also should be noted that real property generally will constitute tax-exempt use property only where more than 35 percent of the property is leased to tax-exempt entities in disqualified leases. The phrase "more than 35 percent of the property" means more than 35 percent of the net rentable floor space of the property, exclusive of common areas.[17] However, in listing the categories of expenses that do not constitute QREs for purposes of the Historic Tax Credit, the Code includes "any expenditure in connection with the rehabilitation of a building which is allocable to the portion of such property which is (or may reasonably be expected to be) tax-exempt use property (within the meaning of section 168(h), except that '50 percent' shall be substituted for '35 percent' in paragraph (1)(B)(iii) thereof)."[18] Therefore, in the case of the Historic Tax Credit, a 50 percent test rather than a 35 percent test applies. The net rentable floor space in a building does not include the common areas of the building, regardless of the terms of the lease. For purposes of applying this rule, two or more buildings will be treated as separate properties unless they are part of the same project, in which event they will be treated as one property. The treasury regulations state that two or more buildings will be treated as part of the same project "if the buildings are constructed, under a common plan, within a reasonable time of each other on the same site and will be used in an integrated manner."[19]

15 *Id.* § 168(h)(1)(B)(ii).

16 Treas. Reg. § 1.168(j)-1T, A-4 (as amended in 1992).

17 *Id.* at Q&A6.

18 I.R.C. § 47(c)(2)(B)(v).

19 Treas. Reg. § 1.168(j)-1T, A-6 (as amended in 1992). *See also* Priv. Ltr. Rul. 201228015 (July 13, 2012); Priv. Ltr. Rul. 201228016 (July 13, 2012).

The treasury regulations provide guidance on what is included in determining the length of a lease term and make it clear that the term may extend beyond the period stated in the lease.[20]

The treasury regulations also make it clear that a service contract could be considered to be a lease under Code § 7701(e) for purposes of the foregoing rules, stating:

> If a contract which purports to be a service contract is treated as a lease under section 7701(e), such contract is to be treated as a lease for all purposes of Chapter 1 of the Internal Revenue Code (including, for example, section 168(j) and section 48(a)(4) and (5)).[21]

20 Treas. Reg. § 1.168(j)-1T, Q&A 17 (as amended in 1992), states, in relevant part:

> A-17. (i) The lease term starts when the property is first made available to the lessee under the lease. The lease term includes not only the stated duration, but also any additional period of time which is within the "realistic contemplation of the parties at the time the property is first put into service." *Hokanson v. Commissioner*, 730 F.2d 1245, 1248 (9th Cir. 1984). A subsequent period of time is included in the term of the original lease if the circumstances indicate that the parties, upon entering into the original lease, had informally agreed that there would be an extension of the original lease.
>
> (ii) With respect to personal property, the lease term includes all periods for which the tax-exempt lessee or a related party (as defined under I.R.C. § 168(j)(7)) has a legally enforceable option to renew the lease, or the lessor has a legally enforceable option to compel its renewal by the tax-exempt entity or a related party. This is true regardless of the renewal terms of the lease agreement or whether the lease is in fact renewed.
>
> (iii) With respect to real property, the lease term includes all periods for which the tax-exempt lessee or a related party (as defined under I.R.C. § 168(j)(7)) has a legally enforceable option to renew the lease, or the lessor has a legally enforceable option to compel its renewal by the tax-exempt entity or a related party, unless the option to renew is at fair market value, determined at the time of renewal. The *Hokanson* facts and circumstances test (see (i) above) may cause the term of a fair market value renewal option to be treated as part of the original lease term.
>
> (iv) Successive leases that are part of the same transaction or a series of related transactions concerning the same or substantially similar property shall be treated as one lease. This rule applies if at substantially the same time or as part of one arrangement the parties enter into multiple leases covering the same or substantially similar property, each having a different term. If so, then the original lease term will be treated as running through the term of the lease that has the last expiration date of the multiple leases. The multiple lease rule will not apply merely because the parties enter into a new lease at fair market rental value at the end of the original lease term.

21 Treas. Reg. § 1.168(j)-1T, A-18 (as amended in 1992). *See* Tidewater Inc. v. United States, 565 F.3d 299 (5th Cir. 2009).

The legislative history of the Tax Reform Act of 1984 indicates that a management contract under which a tax-exempt entity performs services with respect to property owned by another could be considered a lease for purposes of the rules just cited.[22]

In determining the term of a lease, two or more successive leases that are part of the same transaction (or a series of related transactions) with respect to the same or substantially similar property will be treated as one lease.[23] The treasury regulations provide an example to illustrate the application of this rule:

> For example, if one taxable corporation leases property to another taxable corporation for a 20-year term and, as part of the same transaction, the lessee subleases the property to a tax-exempt entity for a 10-year term, then the lease term of the property for purposes of section 168 is 20 years. During the period of tax-exempt use, the property must be depreciated under the alternative depreciation system using the straight line method over the greater of its class life or 25 years (125 percent of the 20-year lease term).[24]

---

22 H.R. Rep. No. 98-432, pt. 2, at 1155–56 (1984), Example (3), which states:

> E, a municipal housing authority, owns section 8-assisted low-income housing projects. E sells the property to T, a partnership of taxable persons. In order to ensure that the purposes of the section 8 housing program are fulfilled, T retains E to manage the property under a long-term management contract. Under the management contract, E performs many of the same managerial and administrative functions that it performed before the sale. However, T exercises a degree of control over E's activities, by virtue of provisions in the management contract that require E to keep adequate records of its operations, to use its best efforts to lease the housing units, and to pay net earnings to T within a reasonable time period. For these services, E is compensated by a fee determined on an arm's-length basis. T bears the risk that the property will decline in value and that the property will be damaged or lost. E does not have an option to repurchase the property.
>
> The mere fact that E continues to control the maintenance and operation of the property under a management contract does not provide a basis for treating the contract as a lease under the service contract provision of the bill. However, the bill leaves open the possibility that an arrangement structured as a management contract could be treated as a lease (under which the tax-exempt entity provides services to third parties for its own benefit) under present law rules. *See McNabb v. Commissioner*, 81-1 USTC 9143 (W.D. Wash. 1980) (where an arrangement structured as a management contract was characterized as a lease because the taxpayer did not adequately control the venture and did not bear the risk of loss); *Meagher v. Commissioner*, 36 T.C.M. 1091 (1977) (where the court held that an agreement was a management contract and not a lease, applying the same tests discussed in the *McNabb* case).

23 I.R.C. § 168(i)(3)(A)(ii).

24 Treas. Reg. § 1.168(i)-2(c).

Under the provisions of the treasury regulations, additional periods of time will be included in a lease term if

> the lessee (or a related person) has (i) agreed that one or both of them will or could be obligated to make a payment of rent or a payment in the nature of rent with respect to such period; or (ii) has assumed or retained any risk of loss with respect to the property for such period (including, for example, by holding a note secured by the property).[25]

7.2.2 Examples

The following examples (which are derived from the legislative history of the tax-exempt use rules) illustrate the application of such rules.

7.2.2.1 Example One

Assume that a governmental unit issues tax-exempt bonds, the proceeds of which are used by a partnership to acquire an existing building from a third party. The building is listed in the National Register. None of the partners of the partnership is a tax-exempt entity. The partnership rehabilitates the building using other funds and leases 100 percent of the improved building to the governmental unit. Under these facts, the governmental unit is treated under Code § 168(h)(1)(B)(ii)(I) as having participated in the tax-exempt financing of the entire property (including the rehabilitation improvements). As a result, the partnership's lease to the governmental unit is deemed to be a disqualified lease, 100 percent of the property will be treated as tax-exempt use property, and no Historic Tax Credit will be available.

7.2.2.2 Example Two

Assume instead that the acquisition of the building is financed with tax-exempt bonds issued by the same governmental unit. The other facts are the same except that the partnership leases the improved property to an unrelated tax-exempt entity instead of to the governmental unit. Prior to the issuance of the tax-exempt bonds, the tax-exempt entity committed to lease space in the completed building. Under these facts, based on the legislative history of the applicable provisions, the tax-exempt entity will be deemed to have participated in the bond financing, and the result will be the same as in the preceding paragraph.[26] If, on the other hand, the unrelated tax-exempt entity did not commit to lease

25 Treas. Reg. § 1.168(i)-2(b).

26 H.R. Rep. No. 98-432, at 1145 (2d. Sess. 1984).

space in the building prior to the issuance of the bonds, the term of the lease and the percentage of space leased will determine the nature and scope of the tax-exempt use property. For example, if only 40 percent of the net rentable floor space is leased to the tax-exempt entity, no portion of the otherwise eligible expenses will be disallowed as qualified rehabilitation expenditures since Code § 168(h)(1)(B)(iii), as modified by Code § 47(c)(2)(B)(v), substitutes a 50 percent test for the 35 percent threshold generally applicable to the determination of whether property constitutes tax-exempt use property. Similarly, even if 100 percent of the completed building is leased to the tax-exempt entity, no portion of the Historic Tax Credit will be disallowed under the tax-exempt use rules if the term of the lease is 20 years or less and no other indicia of a disqualified lease are present.

Note that under the facts in the preceding paragraph, other provisions of the lease could mandate a different result even if the term is less than 20 years. For example, assume that the term of the lease is 15 years, but the lease provides that if the lessee cancels or fails to renew the lease or if the building is destroyed, the lessee will pay or cause to be paid to the partnership, as lessor, the difference between the amount necessary to preserve the lessor's net economic return and the fair market value of the building. Under these circumstances, the lease will be deemed to have a fixed or determinable price purchase or sale option. Accordingly, if more than 50 percent of the net rentable space in the building is covered by the lease, that percentage of the expenses will not constitute QREs eligible for the Historic Tax Credit.

7.3 PROPERTY OWNED BY PARTNERSHIPS WITH TAXABLE AND TAX-EXEMPT PARTNERS

The Code sets forth a number of specific rules intended to prevent the use of tiered arrangements or partnerships and other pass-through entities to allocate in a disproportionate manner the tax benefits and burdens of property owned by tax-exempt entities. In general, if any property that is not otherwise treated as tax-exempt use property is owned by a partnership that has both tax-exempt and taxable partners, the "proportionate share" of the property allocated to the tax-exempt partners will be treated as tax-exempt use property unless the allocations of partnership items to the tax-exempt partner constitute "qualified allocations" or unless such portion of the property is predominantly used by the tax-exempt partner or partners, through the partnership, in an unrelated trade or business the income from which is subject to taxation under Code § 511.[27]

For purposes of applying the foregoing rules, a "tax-exempt controlled entity" is treated as a tax-exempt entity. The effect of this rule is to subject partnerships

27 I.R.C. § 168(h)(6)(A).

(and other pass-through entities to be described in future treasury regulations) to the tax-exempt use property rules where a partnership interest is owned by a taxable corporation that is substantially owned by tax-exempt or foreign persons. A tax-exempt controlled entity is defined as any corporation (that does not otherwise constitute a tax-exempt entity determined without regard to the provisions of Code § 168(h)(6)(F)(iii)(I) and Code § 168(h)(2)(E), which treats certain previously tax-exempt organizations or successors of tax-exempt organizations as continuing to be exempt), if 50 percent or more (in value) of the stock in that corporation is held by one or more tax-exempt entities (other than a foreign person or entity).[28] For purposes of applying this 50 percent ownership test, the attribution rules of Code § 318 will be applied, except that there is no 50 percent limitation for purposes of applying the provisions of Code § 318(a)(2)(C) (i.e., a tax-exempt entity will be deemed to own its proportionate share of the stock owned by any corporation in which it is a shareholder, without regard to whether the tax-exempt entity owns 50 percent or more of that corporation's stock).

One approach to avoiding the application of the tax-exempt entity leasing rules to a project owned by a partnership is to ensure that the partnership agreement contains "qualified allocations." An allocation constitutes a qualified allocation if it is consistent with the allocation to the tax-exempt partner of the same share of the partnership's income, gain, loss deduction, credit, and basis during the entire period in which the tax-exempt entity is a partner. In addition, the allocation must have substantial economic effect as required under Code § 704(b). The only varying allocations that are permitted are those described in Code § 704(c) that apply in the event of an actual contribution of property by a partner to the partnership.[29]

If any allocation to a tax-exempt partner does not constitute a qualified allocation, the tax-exempt partner's "proportionate share" of the partnership's property is equal to that partner's highest percentage share of any item of partnership income or gain (excluding gain allocated under Code § 704(c)).[30] Any portion of the partnership's property that is determined to be tax-exempt use property under these rules must be depreciated over the extended recovery period described earlier and will not be eligible for the Historic Tax Credit. In some syndicated transactions, the general partner or managing member (which is likely to be the tax-exempt partner) will have only a 1 percent (or even a lesser percentage) "bottom line" interest in the profits, losses, and distributions of the partnership. Accordingly, even if the allocations set forth in the partnership agreement are determined not to be "qualified allocations," the impact of the tax-exempt entity leasing rules would be limited to a disallowance of the

28 *Id.* § 168(h)(6)(F)(iii)(I).

29 *Id.* § 168(h)(6)(B); Treas. Reg. § 1.168(j)-1T, Q&A 22(i) (as amended in 1992).

30 I.R.C. § 168(h)(6)(C).

Historic Tax Credit with respect to only 1 percent (or any applicable lesser percentage) of the QREs and extended depreciation for the same small portion. However, in other transactions, the general partner or managing member is allocated a higher residual share of profits (from a sale of the project, etc.) than its share of operating profits. In those cases, the impact of the tax-exempt use rules on cost recovery periods and the use of the Historic Tax Credit could be significant.[31]

The Code provides that a tax-exempt controlled for-profit entity that is a member of a partnership can elect not to be treated as a tax-exempt entity.[32] If such an election is made, however, any gain recognized by a tax-exempt entity shareholder of such tax-exempt controlled entity upon the disposition of the stock in the corporation, and any dividends (to the extent not already subject to tax) or interest received by the tax-exempt shareholder from the controlled corporation, will forever be treated as unrelated business taxable income (UBTI) to the shareholder and will be subject to tax under Code § 511.

It is important to note that a Code § 168(h)(6)(F) election is irrevocable and will bind all tax-exempt entities that are shareholders of the tax-exempt controlled entity for all future years with respect to gain, dividends, and interest paid or distributed by the tax-exempt controlled entity to its parent organization from any and all activities of the tax-exempt controlled entity. It should be emphasized that dividends paid by the tax-exempt controlled entity to its parent organization from income that is taxed at the tax-exempt controlled entity level will not be UBTI to its parent organization since it is already taxed at the tax-exempt controlled entity level. However, if the tax-exempt controlled entity receives cash distributions that are not taxed at the tax-exempt controlled entity level, distributions of these amounts to the parent organization will be treated as UBTI.

Some historic buildings are owned or leased by partnerships or LLCs in which the general partner or managing member is a corporation formed by a housing authority or other governmental agency. If such corporation performs the functions of a government instrumentality, it will be treated as a tax-exempt entity under Code § 168(h)(2)(A) and cannot make a Code § 168(h)(6)(F) election unless it satisfies the safe harbor set forth in Code § 168(h)(2)(D). The safe harbor will be satisfied if the corporation does not file for exemption under Code § 501(c), and the housing authority or other agency does not have the right to select or appoint a majority of its board of directors. In the case of a limited liability company that elects corporate status but has no board of directors, presumably the agency could not have the ability to appoint the managing member or manager of the company. If the safe harbor is satisfied, the corporation will

31 Similarly, qualified allocations would not be an option in a "flip" partnership structure of the type described in Rev. Proc. 2014-12, which is discussed in more detail in Chapter Twelve.

32 I.R.C. § 168(h)(6)(F)(ii).

not be a tax-exempt entity, but it will be a tax-exempt controlled entity, as previously described. Logic would suggest that it should have the ability to make a Code § 168(h)(6) election, although the fact that the parent agency is technically not subject to Code § 511 creates some uncertainty.

What if the corporation formed by the housing authority is exempt from tax under Code § 501(c)(3)? By definition, it would not satisfy the safe harbor in Code § 168(h)(2)(D) and, since it is a tax-exempt entity, it cannot make a Code § 168(h)(6)(F) election. However, if it forms a taxable subsidiary that is not directly or indirectly controlled by the housing authority, the subsidiary should be able to make a valid Code § 168(h)(6)(F) election since the first-tier exempt entity would be subject to tax on UBTI under Code § 511.

In short, the potential adverse impact of having an exempt organization serve as a general partner (or managing member) of a partnership or LLC eligible for the Historic Tax Credit can be minimized either by insuring that the allocations of tax items in the partnership or operating agreement constitute qualified allocations or by having the tax-exempt entity set up a for-profit subsidiary as a "blocker" entity and making an election under Code § 168(h)(6)(F). Of course, the tax-exempt organization will need to evaluate the economic impact of using a blocker entity that makes the Code § 168(h)(6)(F) election. In addition, if the tax-exempt entity is a governmental agency or instrumentality, the special rules set forth in Code § 168(h) relating to instrumentalities will need to be considered.

7.3.1 Other Limitations Applicable to Exempt Entities

Although not directly relevant to the Historic Tax Credit, the Code also generally limits deductions arising from leases and certain other arrangements involving tax-exempt entities, governmental authorities, and foreign persons to the income arising from the property during the term of the lease or other arrangement.[33] A discussion of these provisions is beyond the scope of this book.

33 *Id.* § 470.

Chapter Eight

Partnership Allocation and Basis Reduction Rules

8.1 GENERAL RULES

Most buildings that are eligible for the Historic Tax Credit are owned by limited partnerships or LLCs that are taxed as partnerships for federal income tax purposes. In general, allocations by a partnership of profits, losses, and other tax items to a partner will be respected only if such allocations have substantial economic effect within the meaning of Code § 704(b) and the Code § 704(b) treasury regulations. In order for an allocation to have an economic effect that is substantial, it must satisfy a series of rules and conditions described in great detail in the Code § 704(b) treasury regulations.[1] Among other things, the Code § 704(b) treasury regulations require adjustments to the capital account of each partner to ensure that such partner actually will receive the economic benefit of any income and the economic detriment of any loss allocated to such partner.

The Code § 704(b) treasury regulations provide that allocations of tax credits and tax credit recapture cannot have economic effect because such allocations do not affect a partner's capital account. Consequently, such allocations will be respected only if they are in accordance with a partner's interest in the partnership at the time the tax credits or tax credit recapture arises.

As noted in the Summary of Contents in the 2020 treasury regulations discussed in Chapter Ten,[2] the Historic Tax Credit itself is not allocated by the partnership. Instead, the partnership allocates the QREs to its partners, who then claim the credit at the partner level. In this regard, the treasury regulations provide that each partner's share of the partnership's "section 38 property" (which includes QREs eligible for the Historic Tax Credit) is determined in accordance with the ratio in which the partners divide the general profits of the partnership pursuant to Code § 702(a)(8) (Former Code § 702(a)(9)), regardless of whether the partnership has profits or losses during the taxable year in which the investment tax credit property is placed in service.[3] Where the ratio in which the partners divide the

1 *See* Treas. Reg. § 1.704-1(b)(2).

2 *See* Section 10.2.2.

3 Treas. Reg. § 1.46-3(f)(2)(i).

general profits of the partnership changes during the taxable year of the partnership, the ratio effective for the date on which the property is placed in service shall apply. When a partner intends to make a qualified progress expenditure election, such partner's share of qualified progress expenditures will be determined in the same manner as provided in Treas. Reg. § 1.46-3(f)(2)(i), except that if the ratio in which general profits are allocated changes during the taxable year, the ratio effective on the date on which the qualified progress expenditures are paid or chargeable to capital account (as applicable) applies.[4] General profits represent the taxable income of the partnership, excluding any items subject to a special allocation (described in Code § 702(a)(1) through 702(a)(7)) under the partnership agreement that differs from the general allocation of partnership taxable income. In addition to various other items, gains and losses from sales or exchanges of capital assets or property described in Code § 1231 (relating to certain property used in a trade or business and involuntary conversions) are excluded from general, or "bottom line," profits.[5] The treasury regulations state that allocations in accordance with Treas. Reg. § 1.46-3(f) are deemed to be made in accordance with the partners' interests in the partnership.[6]

There is no definitive guidance on how to determine a partner's share of bottom-line profits when profits from a capital transaction (such as a sale of the project owned by the partnership) are allocated in a different manner than normal operating profits. Since the treasury regulations focus on the share of profits in effect on the date on which the property is placed in service, a compelling argument can be made that the operating profit percentage should apply. This conclusion is buttressed by several points. In the first place, as noted earlier, the applicable provisions of the treasury regulations refer to the *general* profits of the partnership as reflected in Former Code § 702(a)(9) (now Code § 702(a)(8)). Code § 702(a)(8) requires reporting as a separate category the "taxable income or loss, *exclusive of items requiring separate computation under other paragraphs of this subsection*" (emphasis added). As previously discussed, capital gains and losses, as well as Code § 1231 gains, are required to be taken into account under other specific paragraphs of Code § 702(a). The gain from the sale of a syndicated project would fall within one of these specifically enumerated categories. The "general profits" approach also is reflected in Schedule K-1 of Form 1065 (Partner's Share of Income, Credits, Deductions, etc.) as "other income (loss) (attach schedule)." If any "other income" is recognized by a partnership claiming the Historic Tax Credit in the year in which the rehabilitation improvements are placed in service, it almost certainly will be allocated either under Code § 702(a)(8) or under Code § 702(a)(7), which refers to "other items of income, gain, loss, deduction, or credit, to the extent provided by regulations prescribed by the

4 *Id.* § 1.46-5(p)(2).
5 I.R.C. § 702(a)(1)–(3).
6 Treas. Reg. § 1.704-1(b)(4)(ii).

Secretary." Because of the sale restrictions typically imposed in such transactions, as discussed in the next paragraph, it is highly unlikely that the residual sharing percentages set forth in a syndicated partnership agreement ever would apply in the year in which the Historic Tax Credit is claimed.

Second, the treasury regulations provide that where the general profits ratio changes during a taxable year, the ratio in effect when the property (i.e., the rehabilitation improvements) is placed in service applies. A similar rule applies to qualified progress expenditures. In a syndicated transaction, it is clear that the project will not be sold in the year of placement in service since such a sale would result in the disallowance or recapture of the entire Historic Tax Credit, which would render the entire investment moot. In fact, most syndicated partnership or operating agreements prohibit such a sale during the five-year recapture period, at least without the consent of the investor.

Notwithstanding the language of the treasury regulations, the IRS indicated in a 1989 private letter ruling that the reference to general profits in Treas. Reg. § 1.46-3(f)(2)(i) is based on the premise that the purported profit-sharing ratio would have substantial economic effect and reflect the real economics of the partners' profit-sharing arrangement.[7] In that ruling, which involved a staged "flip-down" of the investor's profits interest, the IRS ruled that the allocation on which the investment tax credit allocation was based lacked substantiality. The IRS based its ruling on the fact that, in that case, the partnership was not expected to derive bottom-line profits during any taxable year in which the profit allocation on which the credit allocation was based was in effect. In contrast to the situation in the ruling, however, many partnerships or other entities that operate historic rehabilitation projects (either through direct ownership or pursuant to a lease with a Code § 50(d) election) generate bottom-line profits during the period when such allocation is effective. Moreover, "flip" structures in syndicated Historic Tax Credit transactions are now explicitly permitted under the safe harbor in Rev. Proc. 2014-12.[8]

8.2 BASIS REDUCTION

The Code and the treasury regulations provide that if an Historic Tax Credit is allowed with respect to property attributable to QREs incurred in connection with the rehabilitation of a qualified rehabilitated building, the increase in the basis of the rehabilitated property that otherwise would result from such QREs must be reduced by the amount of the Historic Tax Credit. Any such downward

7 Priv. Ltr. Rul. 8931001 (Mar. 15, 1989).

8 *See* Chapter Twelve. *See also* Rev. Proc. 2007-65, 2007-2 C.B. 967 and Rev. Proc. 2020-12, 2020-11 I.R.B.

basis adjustment to property owned by a partnership in turn triggers an equivalent downward adjustment to the aggregate bases of the partnership interests of the partners.[9] The treasury regulations provide that any such downward basis adjustments must be allocated among the partners in the same proportion as the basis of the property is allocated.[10] As discussed in Chapter Ten, the IRS has issued treasury regulations illustrating how the basis adjustment rules are coordinated with the five-year ratable share provisions included in the TCJA and the recapture provisions in Code § 50.[11] The treasury regulations further require that the capital accounts of the partners be adjusted by their shares of any such basis adjustments.[12] In the Summary of Contents in the 2020 treasury regulations, the

9 I.R.C. § 50(c)(5); Treas. Reg. § 1.48-12(e).

10 Treas. Reg. § 1.46-3(f), which states, in relevant part:

> (f) *Partnership.*—(1) *In general.* In the case of a partnership, each partner shall take into account separately, for his taxable year with or within which the partnership taxable year ends, his share of the basis of partnership new section 38 property and his share of the cost of partnership used section 38 property placed in service by the partnership during such partnership taxable year. Each partner shall be treated as the taxpayer with respect to his share of the basis of partnership new section 38 property and his share of the cost of partnership used section 38 property. The estimated useful life to each partner of such property shall be deemed to be the estimated useful life of the property in the hands of the partnership. Partnership section 38 property shall not, by reason of each partner taking his share of the basis or cost into account, lose its character as either new section 38 property or used section 38 property, as the case may be. For computation of each partner's qualified investment for the energy credit for a qualified intercity bus, see Treas. Reg. § 1.48-9(q)(9)(iv).
>
> (2) *Determination of partner's share.*—(i) Each partner's share of the basis (or cost) of any section 38 property shall be determined in accordance with the ratio in which the partners divide the general profits of the partnership (that is, the taxable income of the partnership as described in section 702(a)(9)) regardless of whether the partnership has a profit or a loss for its taxable year during which the section 38 property is placed in service. However, if the ratio in which the partners divide the general profits of the partnership changes during the taxable year of the partnership, the ratio effective for the date on which the property is placed in service shall apply.
>
> (ii) Notwithstanding subdivision (i) of this subparagraph, if all related items of income, gain, loss, and deduction with respect to any item of partnership section 38 property are specially allocated in the same manner and if such special allocation is recognized under section 704(a) and (b) and paragraph (b) of Treas. Reg. § 1.704-1, then each partner's share of the basis of such item of new section 38 property or the cost of such item of used section 38 property shall be determined by reference to such special allocation effective for the date on which the property is placed in service.

11 *See* Subsection 10.2.2.

12 Treas. Reg. § 1.704-1(b)(2)(iv)(j), which states:

> (j) *Basis adjustments to section 38 property.* The capital accounts of the partners will not be considered to be determined and maintained in accordance with the rules of this paragraph (b)(2)(iv) unless such capital accounts are adjusted by the partners' shares of any upward or downward basis adjustments allocated to them

Treasury Department clarified that the required capital account adjustment does not take into account the five-year credit period. Accordingly, the full amount of the capital account adjustment under Treas. Reg. § 1.704-1 is reflected in a partner's capital account in the year the Historic Tax Credit is determined.

The immediate capital account adjustment raises some interesting issues. Assume, for example, that G and L form a limited partnership to acquire and rehabilitate an existing historic building. G is the GP and has a 1 percent interest in the partnership's profits, losses, and distributions. L is the investor with a 99 percent interest in such items. G contributes $100,000 to the capital of the partnership and L contributes $900,000. The partnership borrows $7 million from an unrelated commercial lender and, using the proceeds of both the equity contributions and the debt, rehabilitates the building. Of the total project costs of $8 million, $5 million constitute QREs, resulting in an Historic Tax Credit of 20 percent of such amount, or $1 million. The loan is recourse to G but not to L. Under the terms of the partnership agreement, 99 percent of the QREs, or $4,950,000 (resulting in a credit of $990,000), is allocated to L in the year in which the rehabilitation improvements are completed and placed in service.

Under these facts, the partnership's basis in the rehabilitated building must be reduced by the $1 million Historic Tax Credit. Similarly, the outside basis and Code § 704(b) capital accounts of G and L must be reduced by their allocable shares of the entire credit, even though it will be claimed ratably over five years. Outside basis cannot be reduced below zero. However, it is possible for a partner to have a negative Code § 704(b) capital account. L's initial capital account is $900,000. The allocation to L of $4,950,000 of QREs (resulting in a $990,000 Historic Tax Credit at the partner level) will cause L to have a negative capital account of $90,000. Since L has no share of minimum gain, in order to avoid an impermissible negative capital account and comply with the Code § 704(b) regulations, it may be necessary for L to incur a deficit restoration obligation to support the allocation of the credit. Alternatively, it may be sufficient if, under the partnership agreement, L is allocated income in an amount sufficient to eliminate such negative capital account as quickly as possible.[13]

---

under this paragraph (b)(2)(iv)(*j*). When there is a reduction in the adjusted tax basis of partnership section 38 property under section 48(q)(1) or section 48(q)(3), section 48(q)(6) provides for an equivalent downward adjustment to the aggregate basis of partnership interests (and no additional adjustment is made under section 705(a)(2)(B)). These downward basis adjustments shall be shared among the partners in the same proportion as the adjusted tax basis or cost of (or the qualified investment in) such section 38 property is allocated among the partners under paragraph (f) of Treas. Reg. § 1.46-3 (or paragraph (a)(4)(iv) of Treas. Reg. § 1.48-8). Conversely, when there is an increase in the adjusted tax basis of partnership section 38 property under section 48(q)(2), section 48(q)(6) provides for an equivalent upward adjustment to the aggregate basis or partnership interests. These upward adjustments shall be allocated among the partners in the same proportion as the investment tax credit from such property is recaptured by the partners under Treas. Reg. § 1.47-6.

13 *See* Treas. Reg. §§ 1.704-1(b)(2)(ii)(c) and 1.704-1(b)(2)(ii)(d).

Chapter Nine

How Can Lessees Use the Historic Tax Credit?

9.1 OVERVIEW OF LEASING RULES

A long-term lessee is entitled to claim the Historic Tax Credit for QREs that it incurs in connection with leasehold improvements to the building if (i) the building is substantially rehabilitated, and (ii) the remaining term of the lease (determined without regard to renewal periods) is greater than the property's recovery period for depreciation (i.e., 27.5 years for residential rental property and 39 years for nonresidential real property under current law).[1]

For purposes of the foregoing rule, property subject to a long-term lease will be treated as having been substantially rehabilitated if the lessee's QREs exceed the sum of (i) the lessee's adjusted basis in its leasehold interest and any leasehold improvements that are structural components of the building, (ii) the adjusted basis of any other leasehold interests in the building, and (iii) the adjusted basis of the lessor in the building.[2]

Note that in order to qualify under the preceding rule, the remaining lease term on the date the rehabilitation is completed (determined without regard to any renewal periods) must be at least equal to the depreciation recovery period for the rehabilitation improvements. If the term of the lease is less than the property's depreciation recovery period, the lessee may still be entitled to claim the Historic Tax Credit for expenditures covered by an election under Code § 50(d) (Former Code § 48(d)), as described in Section 9.2.

If a building subject to a long-term lease is sold prior to being substantially rehabilitated, the lessee must use the new owner's holding period and adjusted basis to determine whether the building has been substantially rehabilitated.[3] On the other hand, the treasury regulations provide that

> if a building is sold *after* the date that a lessee has substantially rehabilitated the building with respect to the original lessor's adjusted basis . . . , the lessee's basis may be determined as of the first day of the 24-month

1 I.R.C. § 47(c)(2)(B)(vi); Treas. Reg. § 1.48-12(c)(7)(v).

2 Treas. Reg. § 1.48-12(b)(2)(iii)(B).

3 *Id.* § 1.48-12(b)(2)(ii)(B).

period selected by the lessee or the first day of the original lessor's holding period, whichever is later, and the transfer of the building will not affect the adjusted basis for purposes of the substantial rehabilitation test.[4]

9.2 CODE § 50(d)(5) ELECTION

In addition to permitting a lessee to claim the Historic Tax Credit for QREs incurred by it under a long-term lease, the Code permits a lessor and lessee to agree to treat the lessee as having incurred all or a portion of the rehabilitation expenditures incurred by the lessor (and therefore to pass the Historic Tax Credit attributable to such expenditures through to the lessee). The use of such an election has been the structure of choice for most large syndicated Historic Tax Credit transactions in recent years.[5]

Several factors contributed to the widespread use of the credit pass-through structure. In the first place, in many instances, particularly those involving larger rehabilitation projects, the building or buildings are owned by a partnership or limited liability company with other investors as members. Since QREs are allocated in accordance with the "bottom line" profit shares of the members of a partnership, it often is difficult to reconcile the tax and economic expectations of a tax equity investor with the requirements of other members who are focused primarily on cash returns from their investment. The use of a lease structure provides more flexibility in addressing the differing goals and expectations of the parties. Second, leasing structures provide certain accounting benefits to institutional investors, a subject that is beyond the scope of this publication. Third, a lessee may be insulated from certain risks that otherwise would apply to the owner of the building(s).

Although the factors described in the preceding paragraph all contributed to the popularity of the credit pass-through structure, the most significant reason for the use of this approach was the tax treatment of the so-called section 50(d) income (i.e., the income in lieu of a basis adjustment) generated in these transactions. Prior to the issuance of treasury regulations in 2019, most syndicated master tenant partnerships treated such income as a partnership tax item that increased the basis and Code § 704(b) capital accounts of the partners by their respective distributive shares of such income, thereby generating a larger capital loss (or a smaller share of gain) upon the disposition of a partner's interest or

4 *Id.* (emphasis added).

5 Former Code § 48(d); I.R.C. § 50(d); Treas. Reg. § 1.48-4. Although, as a technical matter, a Code § 50(d) election results in the lessee being treated as having acquired the section 38 property that is the subject of the election (which in the case of an historic building consists of the rehabilitation improvements resulting from the QREs), industry participants consistently have referred to such provision as "passing through" the Historic Tax Credit to the lessee (or its partners or members) and such terminology generally is used throughout this book.

the liquidation of the master tenant partnership. As discussed in more detail in Subsection 9.4.3, the IRS closed this perceived "loophole" in 2019 by the issuance of regulations taking the position that Code § 50(d) income was a partner level rather than a partnership level tax item. While this position had an adverse impact on tax equity pricing in Historic Tax Credit transactions, the master lease structure is still widely used, particularly in situations where other tax credits (such as state historic or state or federal new market or low-income housing credits) are involved or where lenders are willing to provide a subordination, non-disturbance, and attornment agreement but not a foreclosure forbearance agreement. Moreover, as noted earlier, the existence of other investors in the ownership entity often makes the direct admission of a Historic Tax Credit investor to that entity problematic.

Prior to its repeal in 1990, Former Code § 48(d) provided:

> (d) CERTAIN LEASED PROPERTY.—
>
> (1) GENERAL RULE.—A person (other than a person referred to in section 46(e)(1)) who is a lessor of property may (at such time, in such manner, and subject to such conditions as are provided by regulations prescribed by the Secretary) elect with respect to any new section 38 property (other than property described in paragraph (4)) to treat the lessee as having acquired such property for an amount equal to—
>
> (A) except as provided in subparagraph (B), the fair market value of such property, or
>
> (B) if the property is leased by a corporation which is a component member of a controlled group (within the meaning of section 38(c)(3)(B)) to another corporation which is a component member of the same controlled group, the basis of such property to the lessor.

Code § 50(d) provides that, "for purposes of this subpart, rules similar to the rules of the following provisions (as in effect on the day before the date of the enactment of the Revenue Reconciliation Act of 1990) shall apply: . . . (5) Section 48(d) (relating to certain leased property)." Accordingly, the election described in Former Code § 48(d) continues to be available. For federal income tax purposes, Former Code § 48(d) creates the legal fiction that the lessee has purchased the property from the lessor at its fair market value, resulting in the ability of the lessee to take the investment tax credit attributable to the lessor's basis in the property.[6]

6 Treas. Reg. § 1.48-4(a)(1).

The election is available with respect to property that is attributable to QREs described in Code § 47.[7]

In order to qualify for the election under Code § 50(d) (Former Code § 48(d)), the following conditions must be satisfied:

(i) The property must be "section 38 property" in the hands of the lessor; that is, it must be property with respect to which depreciation (or amortization in lieu of depreciation) is allowable to the lessor, and it must satisfy the other requirements set forth in Treas. Reg. § 1.48-1.
(ii) The property must be "new section 38 property" (within the meaning of Treas. Reg. § 1.48-2) in the hands of the lessor, and the original use of such property must commence with the lessor.
(iii) The property must be such that it would have constituted "new section 38 property" to the lessee if such lessee had actually purchased the property.
(iv) A statement of election to treat the lessee as a purchaser must be filed in the manner described in the treasury regulations.
(v) The lessor cannot be a mutual savings bank, cooperative bank, or certain other types of entities.[8]

As noted previously, the Code incorporates the rules of Former Code § 48(d) (as in effect on the day before the date of enactment of the Revenue Reconciliation Act of 1990).[9] One of the requirements for a Code § 50(d) election is that the property must be "section 38 property."[10] Although property used by an organization exempt from tax generally is not section 38 property, property used predominantly in an unrelated trade or business the income of which is subject to tax under Code § 511 is section 38 property.[11] If the property is debt-financed property as defined in Code § 514(b), the basis or cost of such property for purposes of computing the qualified investment includes only that percentage of the basis or cost that is the same percentage as is used under Code § 514(a), for the year the property is placed in service, in computing the amount of gross income to be taken into account during such taxable year with respect to such property.[12] The term "property used by an organization" means (i) property owned by the organization (whether or not leased to another person) and (ii) property leased to the organization.[13]

7 *Id.* § 1.48-12(f).
8 *Id.* § 1.48-4(a)(1).
9 I.R.C. § 50(d)(5).
10 Treas. Reg. § 1.48-4(a)(1)(i).
11 *Id.* § 1.48-1(j).
12 *Id.*
13 *Id.*

Because property must be new section 38 property in the hands of the lessor and the election is not available unless the lessee is the "original user of the property," it is important to focus on the definition of "original user." The treasury regulations provide:

> [T]he lessor and the lessee may both be considered as the original users of an item of leased property . . . [t]he lessee would not be considered the original user of the property if it has been previously used by the lessor or another person. . . . However, the lessee would be considered the original user if he is the first person to use the property for its intended function. Thus, the fact that the lessor may have, for example, tested, stored, or attempted to lease the property to other persons will not preclude the lessee from being considered the original user.[14]

It is important to note the distinction between the placed-in-service rules discussed in Chapter Three and the original user rules. The treasury regulations provide that for purposes of the credit allowed by Code § 38 (which includes the Historic Tax Credit), property shall be considered placed in service in the *earlier* of (i) the taxable year in which, under the taxpayer's depreciation practice, the period for depreciation with respect to such property begins or (ii) the taxable year in which the property is placed in a condition or state of readiness and availability for a specifically assigned function, whether in a trade or business, in the production of income, in a tax-exempt activity, or in a personal activity.[15] A special rule treats property as to which a Code § 48(d) (currently Code § 50(d)(5)) election is made as placed in service by the lessor in the year in which possession is transferred to the lessee. In contrast to the placed-in-service rules, the lease election rules employ an *actual use* standard rather than a standard based on the readiness of the property for its intended function. That is, as long as the lessee is the first person to "use" the property, the lessee will be treated as the original user of the property.

9.3 SHORT-TERM LEASES

Special rules apply where a lessee occupies the property under a "short-term" lease. A short-term lease is defined as a lease for less than 80 percent of the class life of the property.[16] In the case of a short-term lease, the treasury regulations limit the Historic Tax Credit available to the lessee to its "qualified investment."[17]

14 *Id.* § 1.48-4(b).
15 *Id.* § 1.46-3(d)(1).
16 *Id.* § 1.48-4(a)(2).
17 *Id.* § 1.48-4(c)(3).

The lessee's qualified investment is determined by multiplying the fair market value of the leased premises by a fraction, "the numerator of which is the term of the lease and the denominator of which is the class life of the property leased."[18] However, if the term of the lease is less than 80 percent of the property's class life, the lease will not be considered short term if the lease constitutes a "net lease (within the meaning of section 57(c)(1)(B) (as in effect on the day before the date of enactment of the Tax Reform Act of 1986))."[19]

Options to renew are not taken into account in calculating the lease term. It is important to note, however, that the treasury regulations do not require that the lessee be obligated to occupy the leased premises for the entire term of the lease or that the lease be non-assignable or non-terminable. Instead, the treasury regulations provide that a lease will be treated as binding for its stated term so long as cancellation of the lease would result in a "substantial penalty upon the lessee."[20] These treasury regulations further provide that "[g]enerally, a penalty equal to 25 percent of the total remaining rental payments due under the lease will be regarded as substantial."[21]

There is some uncertainty concerning how to apply the short-term lease rules to real property under present law, particularly in view of the statement in Code § 50(d)(5) that "rules similar to the rules of . . . Section 48(d) . . . (as in effect on the day before the date of the enactment of the Revenue Reconciliation Act of 1990)" shall apply. The "less than 80 percent" requirement was contained in Former Code § 48(d)(4). The old treasury regulations provided as follows:

> The class life of property shall be determined under section 167(m) and the regulations prescribed in connection with that section, except that such class life shall be determined without regard to any variance from the class life permitted under such section. If a class life has not been prescribed for property under section 167(m) on the date such property is leased, the class life of such property shall be the estimated useful life used to compute the allowance for depreciation with respect to such property under section 167.[22]

Prior to the introduction of the accelerated cost recovery system (ACRS) in 1981, depreciation was governed by the provisions of Code § 167. In order to calculate depreciation deductions, it was necessary to determine the useful life

18 *Id.* § 1.48-4(c)(3).

19 I.R.C. § 48(d)(4)(2)(D), *repealed by* Pub. L. No. 101-508, 104 Stat. 1388-1, 536–59 (1990), and Treas. Reg. § 1.48-4(a)(2).

20 Treas. Reg. § 1.48-4(a)(2).

21 *Id.*

22 *Id.*

of the asset that was being depreciated. In 1942 and 1962, the IRS issued tables containing estimated or "guideline" useful lives for tangible depreciable assets, which were replaced in 1971 by the so-called asset depreciation range (ADR) system, which assigned a "class life" to most depreciable property. The ADR system was in turn replaced in 1981 by ACRS, which required taxpayers to recover the cost of tangible assets over statutorily fixed cost recovery periods. The 1981 rules were amended several times, most notably in 1986 with the introduction of the modified accelerated recovery system (MACRS).

Under current law, depreciation deductions provided by Code § 167(a) for tangible property generally are determined under Code § 168. Code § 168 sets forth two methods for determining depreciation or cost recovery deductions: (i) the general depreciation system described in Code § 168(a) and (ii) the alternative depreciation system described in Code § 168(g). Under both of these methods, depreciation is calculated based on prescribed depreciation or cost recovery methods and conventions. For purposes of both Code § 168(a) and Code § 168(g), the applicable recovery period is determined by reference to class life or by statute.

The term "class life" is defined in Code § 168(i)(1) as the class life, if any, that would have applied to the property under Former Code § 167(m) (determined without regard to Code § 167(m)(4) and as if the taxpayer had made an election under Code § 167(m)), as in effect on the day before the date of enactment of the Revenue Reconciliation Act of 1990. Before it was revoked, Code § 167(m) provided that a taxpayer who elected the ADR system of depreciation based depreciation deductions on the class life prescribed by the Treasury that reasonably reflected the anticipated useful life of the property to the relevant industry or group.

The treasury regulations set forth detailed rules for classifying assets under Former Code § 167(m).[23] In general, the classification of property depends on its primary use, even if the activity in which the property is used is insubstantial compared to all of the taxpayer's activities.

Rev. Proc. 87-56 sets forth the class lives of property subject to depreciation under Code § 168 and establishes two broad categories of depreciable assets: (i) specific assets that are used in all business activities and (ii) assets that are used in specific business activities. Neither residential rental nor nonresidential real property has been assigned a class life. Code § 168(e)(2)(B) defines the term "nonresidential real property" to mean section 1250 property that is not residential rental property (as defined in Code § 168(e)(2)(A)), or property with a class life of less than 27.5 years. The term "residential rental property" means any building or structure if 80 percent or more of the gross rental income from such building or structure for the taxable year is "rental income from dwelling units."

23 *Id.* § 1.167(a)-11(b)(4)(iii)(b) (as amended in 1995).

Nonresidential real property has a recovery period of 39 years for purposes of Code § 168(a) and 40 years for purposes of Code § 168(g). Residential rental property has a recovery period of 27.5 years for purposes of Code § 168(a) and 30 years for purposes of Code § 168(g).[24]

The alternative depreciation system described in Code § 168(g) is mandatory for certain types of property (such as tax-exempt use property) and elective in other cases. Although the recovery period under the alternative depreciation system is generally based on the class life of the applicable property or, if no class life is prescribed, 12 years, the recovery period for both residential and nonresidential real property is not based on any concept of "class life" but is statutorily set at 40 years (in the case of nonresidential real property) or 30 years (in the case of residential rental property). In the case of such real property, alternative depreciation may be elected on a property-by-property basis.

Since "rules similar to" Former Code § 48(d) are supposed to apply and since, under current law, neither residential rental property nor nonresidential real property has a "class life" and each is subject to a statutorily mandated recovery period, most practitioners believe that, in order to avoid the application of the short-term lease provisions of Treas. Reg. § 1.48-4, the term of a lease involving real property must be at least 80 percent of 27.5 years, or 22 years, in the case of residential rental property, and 80 percent of 39 years, or 31.2 years, in the case of nonresidential real property. The MSSP Training Guide explicitly adopts this view in Chapter 15, although it should be noted that the MSSP Training Guide cannot be cited as authority for setting or sustaining a technical position. As already discussed, under certain circumstances the recovery period for real estate under the alternative depreciation system may be extended to 30 years in the case of residential rental property or 40 years in the case of nonresidential real property. However, this will be the case only if tax-exempt use property is involved or if an affirmative election to be subject to alternative depreciation is made. In the absence of such factors, therefore, it would appear that the correct standard for applying the short-term lease provisions in the case of a transaction involving real estate is the applicable MACRS recovery period.

The situation is further complicated by the fact that the TCJA eliminated the separate definitions of "qualified leasehold improvement property," "qualified restaurant property," and "qualified retail improvement property," formerly contained in Code § 168(e) and substituted a new definition of "qualified improvement property."[25] "Qualified improvement property" is defined as any improvement to an interior portion of a building that is nonresidential real property if the improvement is placed in service after the date the building was

24 Rev. Proc. 87-56, 1987-2 C.B. 674, as clarified and modified by Rev. Proc. 88-22, 1988-1 C.B. 785.

25 I.R.C. § 168(e)(6)(A).

first placed in service except for any improvement for which the expenditure is attributable to (i) enlargement of the building, (ii) any elevator or escalator, or (iii) the internal structural framework of the building. The improvements do not need to be made pursuant to a lease.[26] The legislative history of the TCJA makes it clear that Congress intended that the new category of qualified improvement property would be subject to a 15-year recovery period.[27] However, although the original TCJA statutory language defined qualified improvement property and provided for straight-line depreciation, the intended 15-year recovery period was not reflected in such statutory language. This oversight was corrected by Congress in 2020 in the Coronavirus Aid Relief and Economic Security Act P.L. 116-136 (CARES Act), which retroactively classified qualified improvement property as 15-year property and changed the alternative depreciation system recovery period for such property to 20 years. As a result, qualified improvement property also is eligible for bonus depreciation.[28]

Many commercial historic rehabilitation projects include qualified improvement property. Since expenses for which bonus depreciation is claimed do not constitute QREs (and thus do not generate an Historic Tax Credit), owners of such projects typically elect out of bonus depreciation for qualified improvement property. However, since such property presumably is incorporated in any lease, an issue arises as to how to apply the short-term lease rules in such circumstances since a portion of the property subject to the lease has a 15-year rather than a 39-year recovery period. As a practical matter, the issue probably is moot since most master leases in syndicated commercial historic projects have a term of at least 32 years (i.e., not less than 80 percent of the basic 39-year recovery period for nonresidential real estate), which by definition is well in excess of the 15-year period applicable to qualified improvement property. However, as discussed in Section 9.4, the classification of property as qualified improvement property could have an impact on the treatment of so-called "§ 50(d) income" in historic master lease transactions.

If the term of a lease is less than 80 percent of the class life of the property, the short-term lease limitation will not apply if the lease is a "net lease" within the meaning of Former Code § 57(c)(1)(B). That section provides that a net lease is one in which "the lessor is either guaranteed a specified return or is guaranteed in whole or in part against loss of income."

26 *Id.* § 168(e)(6)(B).

27 Cong. Rep. No. 115-466 (PL 115-97), at 367.

28 *See also* Rev. Proc. 2020-23 and Rev. Proc. 2020-25, which allowed eligible partnerships to file amended returns to reflect this change, instead of having to file an administrative adjustment, and provided additional guidance allowing taxpayers to change the depreciation of qualified improvement property placed in service in a tax year ending in 2018, 2019, or 2020.

There is not much legal authority interpreting the language of Former Code § 57(c)(1)(B). The treasury regulations provide:

> [T]he return test is based upon an analysis of the leasing arrangement as a whole in order to determine whether, for any period of time covered by the lease, the lessor is guaranteed a specified return or against loss as a result of the lease. . . . In determining whether the lessor . . . will not suffer a loss as a result of the lease, weight will be given to all the facts and circumstances. . . . A net lease of the type described in this subparagraph will result, for instance, if the lessee is obligated to pay all expenses attributable to the property which the lessor will incur or accrue for a period covered by the lease and, in the event of complete or partial destruction of the property, the lessee is obligated either to continue to pay the full rent for such period or a lump sum amount equivalent to the present value of such rental payments.[29]

The IRS has analyzed the provisions of Former Code § 57(c)(1)(B) in the context of an Historic Tax Credit project in several private letter rulings. The most exhaustive analysis is set forth in a 1989 private letter ruling involving the rehabilitation by a limited partnership of a certified historic structure that the limited partnership leased from a third party under a long-term ground lease.[30] Following the completion of the rehabilitation, the partnership rented out space in the building under a lease that provided for the pass-through of all Historic Tax Credits attributable to the leased space. Shortly thereafter, a corporation purchased the limited partnership's interest in the building, which consisted of its rights under the ground lease, the improvements, and the tenant leases. The corporation then leased this newly acquired property back to the limited partnership. Under the terms of the new lease, the corporation was required to file an election under Former Code § 48(d)(1) to allow the limited partnership to retain the Historic Tax Credits attributable to the rehabilitation. Among other things, the parties requested that the IRS rule that the tenant leases would qualify as net leases under Former Code § 57(c)(1)(B).

The transaction involved several leases. The limited partnership, as lessor, initially executed a lease (First Lessee Lease) covering certain office space. Another lease (Second Lessee Lease) subsequently was executed by the limited partnership in its capacity as lessor. These leases (together, the Lessee Leases) were later amended to provide for the pass-through to the lessee of the Historic Tax Credits, the payment of additional rent to the limited partnership in consideration of such pass-through (ITC Rent), and the payment by the lessee of certain

29 Treas. Reg. § 1.57-3(c).

30 Priv. Ltr. Rul. 8943074 (Aug. 2, 1989).

operating expenses. When the corporation subsequently acquired the limited partnership's interest in the project, the corporation simultaneously leased back to the limited partnership the property purchased by the corporation pursuant to the terms of the master lease between the corporation, as lessor, and the limited partnership, as lessee. Under the terms of this master lease, the Lessee Leases were assigned to the limited partnership so that the limited partnership continued to be the lessor under such leases. The master lease required that the corporation file an election under Former Code § 48(d)(1) in order to ensure that the limited partnership would retain the Historic Tax Credits.

The effect of the master lease on the Lessee Leases was that each was converted to a sublease, and the limited partnership was itself a lessee/sublessor.

The master lease specifically provided that it would be a net lease and that the rent payable by the limited partnership would be due and payable in all events notwithstanding any damage or destruction of the property, any taking or condemnation, eviction, a default by the lessor, a foreclosure on the lessor's interest, or any other reason.

Under the foregoing facts, a critical issue was whether the Lessee Leases constituted net leases. If they did, the Historic Tax Credit allocable to the property subject to such leases could be passed through to the lessee without reduction or limitation.

In addressing the net lease issue, the IRS considered a number of factors. At the outset, the IRS reviewed Prop. Reg. § 1.57-3(c)(2), which enumerated the factors for determining what would constitute a net lease under Former Code § 57(c)(1)(B). The proposed regulations provided, in part, that in determining whether a lessor is assured of a specified return or such lessor will not suffer a loss as a result of the lease, weight must be given to all the facts and circumstances of each case. As a result, an arrangement whereby the lessor is assured by, or on behalf of, the lessee that, during any period, the income that the lessor will receive or accrue as a result of the lease during such period will exceed the expenses the lessor will pay or accrue that are attributable to such property by a fixed or determinable amount (or that such income will equal such expenses) is a net lease for such period. The IRS noted that the parties requesting the ruling had submitted evidence demonstrating that the limited partnership, in its capacity as a lessor, would have a guaranteed positive economic return from the Lessee Leases. The IRS agreed, holding that the situation appeared to be similar to the example in Prop. Reg. § 1.57-3(c)(2), which states:

> [A] net lease of the type described in this subparagraph will result, for instance, if the lessee is obligated to pay all the expenses attributable to the property that the lessor will incur or accrue for a period covered by the lease and, in the event of complete or partial destruction of the property, the lessee is obligated either to continue to pay the full rent for such period or a lump-sum amount equivalent to the present value of such rental payments.

Because of the use of the conjunctive "and" in the preceding example, the IRS concluded that a true net lease should not only be profitable to the lessor but also should reduce or eliminate the lessor's risk of loss from the transaction.

With respect to the risk of loss issue, the IRS examined the legislative history of Former Code § 57(c)(2)(B), which implied that in a net lease situation, the lessor would have a reduced risk of economic loss. In particular, the legislative history of the 15 percent test imposed by Former Code § 57(c)(1)(A) provided that business expenses of a lessor that were reimbursed by the lessee could not be taken into account for purposes of such test since the lessor generally does not incur any risks with respect to such reimbursed expenses.

Under the analysis of the ruling, the basic question in determining whether a lessor is guaranteed against risk of loss is whether the lessor is assured that the rent (or insurance payments in the case of destruction of the premises) will equal or exceed the lessor's costs. As the IRS stated:

> [W]here the lessee agrees to pay all the expenses (other than interest) of the building, such as property taxes, insurance and operating expenses, the lessor will be considered guaranteed against risk of loss if the rental payments equals or exceeds the lessor's costs (including interest and appreciation on the property) and the lessor is assured that the rental payments or insurance payments will also cover those costs for which the lessor is potentially liable, that is, at risk. With respect to the rental continuation insurance, therefore, the issue is whether payment by the lessee of the premiums on such insurance, that is, such payment is a reimbursed expenditure, adequately protects the lessor from the potential risk of loss and income due to casualty to the property.[31]

In the transaction that was the subject of the ruling, the lessee was required to reimburse the limited partnership for rental continuation insurance. Such insurance covered the cost of rebuilding in the event of the destruction of the premises and included a rental continuation benefit that would guarantee the payment of the remaining rent (including ITC rent) due under the Lessee Leases while the premises were being rebuilt and thereafter until the premises were rented at a rate equal to the rate provided in the Lessee Leases.

In the view of the IRS,

> the use of rental continuation insurance, although not dispositive of a net lease determination, is intended to be a substitute for the requirement that the lessee protect the lessor against potential loss from casualty to the premises by continuing to pay full rent or by payment of the lump-sum present value equivalent. The use of rental continuation

31 *Id.*

insurance must be considered in addition to the lessee's obligation to pay the lessor's expenses associated with the premises.[32]

After reviewing the terms of the limited partnership's rental continuation insurance coverage, the IRS concluded that the limited partnership was guaranteed against loss under the return test in Former Code § 57(c)(1)(B).

It also should be noted that the ruling implies that if a lease ceases to be a net lease after the recapture period has passed (i.e., after 60 months following the final placed-in-service date for any portion of the leased property), the election under Former Code § 48(d) would not be jeopardized.

9.4 SECTION 50(d) INCOME

9.4.1 Income in Lieu of Basis Adjustment

When a lessor makes an election under Code § 50(d)(5) and Treas. Reg. § 1.48-4 to treat the lessee as having acquired the leased property, the general basis adjustment rules described in Chapter Eight do not apply. Instead, the lessee is required to include ratably in gross income, over the shortest recovery period that could be applicable under Code § 168, an amount equal to 100 percent of the Historic Tax Credit.[33]

9.4.2 Example

To illustrate the impact of the foregoing rules, assume that the rehabilitation of a commercial property qualifies as a certified rehabilitation of a certified historic structure and generates an Historic Tax Credit of $2 million. The property is leased to a corporate taxpayer and placed in service in 2023. The lease has a term of 20 years and constitutes a "net lease" within the meaning of Former Code § 57(c)(1)(B). An election is made under Code § 50(d)(5) and Treas. Reg. § 1.48-4 to treat the lessee as the owner of the rehabilitation improvements. The taxpayer/lessee would be entitled to an Historic Tax Credit of $2 million, taken ratably in five equal installments of $400,000 commencing in 2023, that could be used to offset taxes in each of such years (subject, in either case, to the general limitations on the use of tax credits). Since the shortest recovery period for commercial real estate is 39 years, Code § 50(d)(5), as interpreted by the IRS, would require the taxpayer to report $51,282 of income each year for the balance of the 39-year recovery period.[34]

---

32 *Id.*

33 *See* CCA 201505038. Note that the I.R.C. § 50(d) income must be reported on an annual basis even if the taxpayer was unable to use the credit when it was initially available because of the general limitations on the use of credits imposed by I.R.C. § 38. Treas. Reg. § 1.50-1(b)(2)(i).

34 Note that if a portion of the leased property constitutes qualified improvement property, the I.R.C. § 50(d) income attributable to such portion presumably would be reported over 15 years.

9.4.3 How Do the Section 50(d) Income Rules Apply to a Lessee That Is a Partnership?

An interesting technical issue arises when, as normally is the case in a syndicated Historic Tax Credit transaction in which an election is made under Code § 50(d)(5) and Treas. Reg. § 1.48-4, the lessee is a partnership or other pass-through entity. If the building (including the associated rehabilitation improvements) generating the Historic Tax Credit actually was owned by the lessee partnership, the treasury regulations and Code would require the capital accounts and "outside" tax basis of the partners of the partnership to be reduced by any Historic Tax Credit claimed by the lessee partnership.[35] As discussed in Section 9.2, for many years, it was common in syndicated historic master lease transactions to treat the Code § 50(d) income in lieu of a basis adjustment as a partnership tax item that increased the outside basis and capital accounts of the members of the lessee partnership or, in the case of an S corporation, the outside basis of its shareholders in their stock. In the view of the IRS, this approach provided an unintended benefit to such members or shareholders and was inconsistent with the purpose of the income inclusion provisions. In 2019, the IRS issued final treasury regulations clarifying that Code § 50(d) income is not an item of partnership income or S corporation income that is allocated to partners or S corporation shareholders, as the case may be. Instead, each partner or S corporation shareholder that is the ultimate credit claimant is treated as the lessee for purposes of reporting Code § 50(d) income.[36] In the preamble to the treasury regulations, the IRS explained that, because the investment credit and any limitations on the credit itself are determined at the partner or S corporation shareholder level, it is appropriate that the income inclusion occurs at the partner or shareholder level. For example, in the case of a partnership that owns property eligible for the Historic Tax Credit, each partner in the partnership is treated as the taxpayer with respect to the partner's share of the basis of partnership investment credit property (i.e., the improvements funded with the QREs) under Treas. Reg. § 1.46-3(f)(1) and separately computes the Historic Tax Credit (which is an investment credit) based on its share of the partnership's basis in the investment credit property. Similarly, in the case of an historic master lease transaction where the lessor makes an election under Code § 50(d) and Treas. Reg. § 1.48-4 to treat a lessee partnership as having acquired investment credit property, each partner in the lessee partnership is the taxpayer with respect to whom the investment credit is determined for under Code § 46 and must separately compute the investment credit based on such partner's share of the investment credit property. In other words, the credit is computed at the partner level based on partner level limitations. Treas. Reg. § 1.704-1(b)(4)(ii),

35 Treas. Reg. § 1.704-1(b)(2)(iv)(j), (b)(4)(ii) (as amended in 2015); I.R.C. § 50(c)(5).

36 Treas. Reg. § 1.50-1 (effective July 17, 2019).

which requires allocations with respect to the investment tax credit provided by Code § 38 to be made in accordance with the partners' interests in the partnership, provides that allocations of cost or qualified investment (as opposed to the investment credit itself, which is not determined at the partnership level) made in accordance with Treas. Reg. § 1.46-3(f) will be deemed to be made in accordance with the partners' interests in the partnership.

Similar principles apply in the case of a lessor that makes an election under Treas. Reg. § 1.48-4 to treat a lessee S corporation as having acquired investment credit property.

The basic rationale of the IRS and Treasury Department is that the burden of income inclusion should match the benefits of the allowable credit. Since the investment credit and any limitations on the credit are determined at the partner or shareholder level, the treasury regulations reflect the notion that Code § 50(d) income is not an item of partnership income for purposes of subchapter K or an item of S corporation income for purposes of subchapter S. As a result, the basis adjustment rules that would apply if such gross income was an item of income under Code § 702 or Code § 1366, such as Code § 705(a) (providing for an increase in partner's outside basis for items of partnership income) or Code § 1367(a) (providing for an increase in an S corporation shareholder's stock basis for items of S corporation income), do not apply.[37]

The treasury regulations also coordinate the Code § 50(d) income inclusion rules with the credit recapture rules in Code § 50(a). When the investment credit recapture rules under Code § 50(a) are triggered (including when there is a lease termination), causing a recapture of the credit or a portion of the credit, an adjustment will be made to the gross income of the lessee (or, as applicable, the ultimate credit claimant), for any discrepancies between the total amount included in gross income under the Code § 50(d) income inclusion provisions and the total credit allowable after recapture. The adjustment amount is taken into account in the taxable year in which the property is disposed of or otherwise ceases to be investment credit property. The treasury regulations provide rules for when the amount of the unrecaptured credit (that is, the allowable credit after taking into account the recapture amount, or 50 percent of the unrecaptured credit in the case of the energy credit) exceeds the income inclusion, and when the income inclusion exceeds the unrecaptured credit.[38]

The treasury regulations also allow a lessee or an ultimate credit claimant to make an irrevocable election to include in gross income any remaining income required to be taken into account under Treas. Reg. § 1.50-1(b)(2) in the taxable year in which the lease terminates or is otherwise disposed of. In addition, if

37 Preamble to TD 9872, 84 Fed. Reg. 34,775 (July 17, 2019).

38 Note that since the recovery periods for real estate (27.5 or 39 years) are considerably longer than the five-year credit recapture period, additional unrealized I.R.C. § 50(d) income always will be present after a recapture event.

an ultimate credit claimant disposes of its entire direct or indirect interest in a partnership (other than an electing large partnership) or an S corporation, the ultimate credit claimant may irrevocably elect to include in gross income any remaining income required to be taken into account under the treasury regulations in the taxable year of the disposition.[39] This election allows a lessee or an ultimate credit claimant to account for any remaining required gross income inclusion in the taxable year in which the lease terminates or is otherwise disposed of or in which an ultimate credit claimant disposes of its investment.[40]

The election is available only outside of the Code § 50(a) recapture period, and only if the lessee or the ultimate credit claimant was not already required to accelerate the gross income required to be included under Treas. Reg. § 1.50-1(b)(2) because of a recapture event during the recapture period.[41] Moreover, a former partner or S corporation shareholder that no longer owns a direct or indirect interest in the lessee partnership or S corporation may not elect to accelerate the gross income required to be included under the treasury regulations at the time of a termination or disposition of the lease by the lessee partnership or S corporation.[42] Instead, a former partner or S corporation shareholder that is an ultimate credit claimant is required to elect income acceleration in the taxable year that it disposes of its entire interest in a lessee partnership or S corporation.

Interestingly, the regulations do not explicitly state what happens to the Code § 50(d) income if the lessee or ultimate credit claimant does not make an election to accelerate and (i) the lease terminates, (ii) the tax equity investor exercises a put option or otherwise disposes of its interest in the master tenant, leaving the master tenant with only one member (and thus converting the master tenant to a disregarded entity rather than a partnership for tax purposes), and/or (iii) the master tenant entity is liquidated and dissolved. In such a case, the regulatory language and examples suggest that the ultimate credit claimant would continue to report its annual share of the Code § 50(d) income on its tax return through the end of the applicable depreciation recovery period.

As discussed in Chapter Ten, the TCJA made no changes to the Code § 50(a) recapture rules when it revised Code § 47(a) to provide for a five-year credit period in the case of the Historic Tax Credit. Under the amended statutory provisions, for any taxable year during the five-year period commencing with the taxable year in which the qualified rehabilitated building

39 Treas. Reg. § 1.50-1(d).

40 Note that making the one-time election to accelerate the recognition of the unrealized I.R.C. § 50(d) income comes at an economic cost to the taxpayer because of time value of money principles. However, many large corporate or institutional investors do not relish the thought of having to track and report such income over a period of many years. As a result, as a matter of administrative convenience, such investors may choose to make the election. Presumably, the economic hit of doing so would be addressed by an adjustment in the equity pricing for the transaction.

41 Treas. Reg. § 1.50-1(d)(2)(i).

42 *Id.* § 1.50-1(d)(2)(ii).

is placed in service, the Historic Tax Credit for the year is an amount equal to the "ratable share," or 20 percent of the QREs with respect to such building, as allocated ratably to each year during such period. The IRS and Treasury Department have requested comments addressing whether any additional guidance under Code § 50(a) is needed to coordinate the credit recapture rules with the income inclusion and other applicable rules relating to the Historic Tax Credit.

9.4.4 Examples

The treasury regulations contain a series of examples illustrating the application of the preceding rules. The following examples are based on the regulatory examples.

9.4.4.1 Example One

Y owns an existing building that is a certified historic structure eligible for the Historic Tax Credit. Following the rehabilitation of the building, X, a calendar year C corporation, leases the building (which constitutes nonresidential real property) from Y. The qualified rehabilitated building is placed in service on October 1, 2023. Y elects under Treas. Reg. § 1.48-4 to treat X as having acquired the building (including the rehabilitation improvements). X's Historic Tax Credit determined under Code § 47 with respect to such property is $975,000. The shortest recovery period that could be available to the property under Code § 168 is 39 years. Because Y has elected to treat X as having acquired the property, Y does not reduce its basis in the property under Code § 50(c). Instead, X, the lessee of the property, must include ratably in gross income over 39 years an amount equal to the Historic Tax Credit with respect to such property. Under the provisions of the treasury regulations, X's Code § 50(d) income for each of the 39 years beginning with 2023 is $25,000 ($975,000/39-year recovery period).

9.4.4.2 Example Two

The facts are the same as in Example One, except that instead of nonresidential real property, X leases from Y solar energy equipment for which an energy credit under Code § 48 is determined under Code § 46. X's investment credit determined under Code § 46 for 2023 with respect to the property is $975,000. The shortest recovery period that could be available to the property under Code § 168 is five years. X, the lessee of the property, must include ratably in gross income over five years an amount equal to 50 percent of the credit determined under Code § 46 with respect to such property. Under the treasury regulations, X's Code § 50(d) income for each of the five years beginning with 2023 is $97,500 ($487,500/five-year recovery period).

9.4.4.3 Example Three

Y owns an existing building that is a certified historic structure eligible for the Historic Tax Credit. Following the rehabilitation of the building, A and B, calendar year taxpayers, form a partnership, the AB partnership, that leases the building (which constitutes nonresidential real property) from Y. The property is placed in service on October 1, 2023. Y elects, under Treas. Reg. § 1.48-4, to treat the AB partnership as having acquired the property. A's Historic Tax Credit determined under Code §§ 46 and 47 for 2023 is $390,000 and B's Historic Tax Credit determined under Codes §§ 46 and 47 for 2023 is $780,000 with respect to the property. The shortest recovery period that could be available to the property under Code § 168 is 39 years. Because Y has elected to treat the AB partnership as having acquired the property, Y does not reduce its basis in the building under Code § 50(c). Instead, A and B, the ultimate credit claimants, must include the amount of the credit determined with respect to A and B ratably in gross income over 39 years, the shortest recovery period available with respect to such property. Therefore, A and B must include ratably in gross income over 39 years an amount equal to $390,000 and $780,000, respectively. A's Code § 50(d) income for each of the 39 years beginning with 2023 is $10,000 ($390,000/39-year recovery period) and B's is $20,000 ($780,000/39-year recovery period). Because such Code § 50(d) income is not an item of partnership income, the rules under subchapter K applicable to items of partnership income, do not apply with respect to such income. In particular, A and B are not entitled to an increase in the outside basis of their partnership interests under Code § 705(a) and are not entitled to an increase in their capital accounts under Code § 704(b).

9.4.4.4 Example Four

The facts are the same as in Example Three, except that on January 1, 2026, the lease between AB partnership and Y terminates (Y retains ownership of the property), which is a recapture event under Code § 50(a). A's and B's income tax for 2026 is increased under Code § 50(a) by $234,000 and $468,000, respectively (60 percent of $390,000 and $780,000, respectively, assuming that the aggregate decrease in the credits allowed under Code § 38 was the full amount of the investment credits determined as to A and B under Code § 46). Therefore, the amount of the unrecaptured credit as to A and B is $156,000 and $312,000, respectively (40 percent of $390,000 and $780,000, respectively). The amounts that A and B previously included in gross income under Code § 50(d) are $30,000 ($10,000 for each of 2023, 2024, and 2025) and $60,000 ($20,000 for each of 2023, 2024, and 2025), respectively. A and B are required to include in gross income an amount equal to the excess of the credit that is not recaptured ($156,000 and $312,000, respectively) over the total Code § 50(d) income previously realized with respect to the property ($30,000 and $60,000, respectively). Therefore, A and B must include in gross income $126,000 and $252,000, respectively, in the taxable year of the lease termination (2026) in addition to the recapture amounts described earlier.

9.4.4.5 Example Five

The facts are the same as in Example Four, except that instead of nonresidential property, the AB partnership leases from Y solar energy equipment for which an energy credit under Code § 48 is determined under Code § 46. Because the shortest recovery period that could be available to the property under Code § 168 is five years, A and B are required to include ratably in gross income over five years an amount equal to 50 percent of the credit determined under Code § 46 with respect to such property (50 percent of $390,000/5, or $39,000, per year for A, and 50 percent of $780,000/5, or $78,000, per year for B).

The January 1, 2026, lease termination requires A's and B's income tax for 2026 to be increased under Code § 50(a) by $234,000 and $468,000, respectively (60 percent of $390,000 and $780,000, respectively). Therefore, the amount of the unrecaptured credit as to A and B is $156,000 and $312,000, respectively (40 percent of $390,000 and $780,000, respectively). The amounts A and B previously included in gross income are $117,000 ($39,000 for each of 2023, 2024, and 2025) and $234,000 ($78,000 for each of 2023, 2024, and 2025), respectively. A and B are entitled to a reduction in gross income equal to the excess of the total Code § 50(d) income realized ($117,000 and $234,000, respectively) over 50 percent of the amount of the credit that is not recaptured ($78,000 and $156,000, respectively). Therefore, A and B are entitled to a reduction in gross income in the amount of $390,00 and $78,000, respectively, in the taxable year of the lease termination (2026).

9.4.4.6 Example Six

The facts are the same as in Example Three, except that on December 1, 2028, A sells its entire interest to C, and on January 1, 2029, the lease between AB partnership and Y terminates. At the time of the lease termination, B is still a partner in the AB partnership. There is no recapture event under Code § 50(a) because both the lease termination and the disposition of A's interest in the partnership occurred outside of the recapture period.

At the time that A sold its interest in the AB partnership to C, A had previously included $50,000 ($10,000 for each of 2023–2027) in gross income under Code § 50(d). A must continue to include the remaining $340,000 (including $10,000 in 2028) in gross income ratably over the remaining portion of the applicable recovery period of 39 years. Alternatively, A may irrevocably elect to include the remaining $340,000 in gross income in the taxable year that A sold its entire interest in the AB partnership to C (2028). A cannot make this election in the taxable year of the lease termination (2029).

At the time of the lease termination, B had previously included $120,000 ($20,000 for each of 2023–2028) in gross income under Code § 50(d). B must continue to include the remaining $660,000 required in gross income ratably over the remaining portion of the applicable recovery period of 39 years. Alternatively, B may irrevocably elect to include the remaining $660,000 in gross income in the taxable year of the lease termination (2029).

9.5 FAIR MARKET VALUE LIMITATION

It is important to note that when an election is made under Code § 50(d) and Treas. Reg. § 1.48-4, the lessee is treated as having "purchased" the property for its fair market value.[43] The treasury regulations contain an example dealing with "short-term lease property" that assumes that the basis of certain leased property is $10,000 and its fair market value is $12,000. It goes on to calculate the credits allowable to the lessee based on the fair market value of the property and the credits allowable to the lessor based on the lessor's basis in the property.[44]

The treasury regulations contain a special rule that applies to an election under Code § 50(d)(5) to treat a lessee as the purchaser of rehabilitation improvements. Under this special rule, "[f]or purposes of applying section 48(d), the fair market value of section 38 property described in section 48(a)(1)(E) shall be limited to that portion of the lessor's basis in the qualified rehabilitated building that is attributable to qualified rehabilitation expenditures."[45] This language highlights the fact that, as typically was not the case with other property for which the investment tax credit was available (such as equipment), in the case of a qualified rehabilitated building, the "section 38 property" is not the entire building that is being rehabilitated but instead is the improvements arising from a certain class of "expenditures" that were incurred in creating the entire "property" (as such term is used in the conventional sense), that is, the qualified rehabilitated building.[46]

43 Treas. Reg. § 1.48-4(c)(2), which is applicable to the pass-through of any section 38 credit, provides that, with respect to "non-short-term lease" property, the lessee is treated as having acquired the "entire property for an amount equal to the fair market value of such property on the date possession is transferred to the lessee." *See also* Treas. Reg. § 1.48-12(f)(1).

44 Treas. Reg. § 1.48-4(c)(4).

45 *Id.* § 1.48-12(f)(1).

46 This concept arises in a similar context in Treas. Reg. § 1.48-12(f)(3)(ii), which states that "[i]n the case of section 38 property described in I.R.C. § 48(a)(1)(E), the section 38 property is not the building. Instead, the section 38 property is the portion of the basis of the building that is attributable to qualified rehabilitated expenditures."

9.6 TRUE LEASE REQUIREMENT

The availability of an election under Code § 50(d) is dependent upon the classification of the applicable lease as a true lease for federal income tax purposes. There is an abundance of authority concerning the proper characterization of leases for federal income tax purposes. The IRS has issued a number of rulings and other guidance in the area, and the courts have addressed lease characterization issues in numerous cases.[47]

As discussed in Chapter Twelve, most syndicated Historic Tax Credit transactions are structured in a manner intended to comply with the Safe Harbor in Rev. Proc. 2014-12. Since such compliance depends, among other things, on demonstrating that lease terms are commercially reasonable, an IRS challenge to true lease status in such a transaction seems unlikely to succeed.

47 For an excellent comprehensive analysis of lease characterization issues, see Toby Cozart, Bloomberg BNA Tax Management Portfolios 544 T.M. Equipment Leasing: Substance and Form, 545 T.M. Equipment Leasing: Benefits and Burdens.

Chapter Ten

Historic Tax Credit Recapture Rules

10.1 OVERVIEW

As noted earlier, the amendments to Code § 47 contained in the TCJA did not modify the investment credit recapture rules in Code § 50. Under these rules, if property attributable to a rehabilitation is disposed of, or otherwise ceases to be "section 38 property," within five years after such property is placed in service, the taxpayer's tax for the year is increased by an amount equal to the total Historic Tax Credit taken multiplied by the applicable "recapture percentage."[1] The recapture percentage is determined based on the holding period of the property resulting from the QREs (i.e., the rehabilitation improvements). The amount of recapture is reduced by 20 percent for each full year that elapses after such property is placed in service. As a result, 100 percent of the Historic Tax Credit is recaptured if the property is disposed of (or ceases to be section 38 property) less than one year after the property is first placed in service. If such disposition or disqualifying event occurs after one year but before the end of two years, the recapture percentage is 80 percent. If the event occurs after two years but before the end of the third year, the recapture percentage is 60 percent. Such percentage decreases to 40 percent after three years and before the end of four years, to 20 percent after four years and before the end of five years, and to zero after the expiration of the full five-year period.

The recapture rules also apply if a partner's share of the "bottom line" profits of a partnership that owns a rehabilitated building is reduced (for example, by a sale of the partner's interest in the partnership, an amendment to the partnership agreement, or the admission of a new partner). The treasury regulations provide that if a partner's interest in the bottom-line profits of such a partnership is reduced to less than two-thirds of the interest held by the partner when the property was placed in service, the reduction is treated as a disposition of a portion of the property.[2] For example, assume

1 I.R.C. § 50(a). *See* Section 10.2 for a discussion of how the recapture rules are applied and coordinated with the five-year ratable share rules introduced in the TCJA.

2 Treas. Reg. § 1.47-6(a)(2).

that a limited partner has an 80 percent interest in a limited partnership that rehabilitated a certified historic structure and placed it in service on January 1, 2023. The limited partner's share of the Historic Tax Credit is $100,000. On February 1, 2026, which is more than three years after the property was first placed in service, the limited partner's interest in the partnership is reduced to 50 percent, which is less than two-thirds of what it was on the placed-in-service date (i.e., the 50 percent interest is only 62.5 percent (50/80) of the original 80 percent interest). Under these facts, the limited partner is deemed to have disposed of an amount of the property proportional to the percentage of the reduction in the limited partner's interest, or 37.5 percent (30/80). This means that the applicable recapture percentage of 40 percent is applied to $37,500 of the Historic Tax Credit (i.e., 37.5 percent of the limited partner's $100,000 share of the Historic Tax Credit). Accordingly, the limited partner has an increase in tax under Code §50(a) in the amount of $15,000 in 2026.

The treasury regulations provide that, in the case of property for which an election has been made under Code § 50(d)(5) (Former Code § 48(d)) and Treas. Reg. § 1.48-4, a mere disposition by the lessor of property subject to a lease generally will not be considered to be a disposition by the lessee. However, if the lessor makes a disposition of property subject to the lease to a person who could not make a valid election under Treas. Reg. § 1.48-4, the property will be considered to have ceased to be "section 38 property" with respect to the lessee on the date of the disposition. Similarly, if a lease is terminated and the property is transferred by the lessee to the lessor or to any other person, such a transfer is considered to be a disposition by the lessee.[3]

10.2 HOW DO THE RATABLE SHARE, RECAPTURE, AND BASIS ADJUSTMENT RULES WORK TOGETHER?

10.2.1 Overview

As noted earlier, Code § 47(a)(1) provides that for purposes of determining the amount of a taxpayer's investment credit under Code § 46, for any taxable year during the five-year period beginning in the taxable year in which a qualified rehabilitated building is placed in service, the Historic Tax Credit for such taxable year is an amount equal to the "ratable share" for the year. As amended by the TCJA, Code § 47(a)(2) defines the ratable share for any taxable year during the credit period as the amount equal to 20 percent of the QREs with respect to the building, as allocated ratably to each year during the credit period. Code § 47(b)(1), which the TCJA did not amend, provides that QREs with respect to a qualified rehabilitated building are taken into account for the taxable year in which the building is placed in service.

3 *Id.* § 1.47-2(b)(2)(iii).

10.2.2 Regulatory Guidance

In treasury regulations proposed on May 22, 2020, and finalized (without change) effective September 18, 2020, the IRS addressed the mechanics of how the ratable share rules are applied and coordinated with the recapture and basis adjustment rules in Code § 50. Treas. Reg. § 1.47-7(b) generally follows the definition of ratable share in Code § 47(a)(2) but, for clarification, replaces "qualified rehabilitation expenditures" with the term "rehabilitation credit determined" as defined in Treas. Reg. § 1.47-7(c). Accordingly, Treas. Reg. § 1.47-7(b) defines the term "ratable share" as the amount equal to 20 percent of the Historic Tax Credit determined with respect to the qualified rehabilitated building, as allocated ratably to each taxable year during the five-year credit period. Treas. Reg. § 1.47-7(c) defines the term "rehabilitation credit determined" as the amount equal to 20 percent of the QREs, as defined in Code § 47(c)(2) and Treas. Reg. § 1.48-12(c), taken into account under Code § 47(b)(1) for the taxable year in which the qualified rehabilitated building is placed in service. However, if the taxpayer claims the additional first-year deprecation for the QREs pursuant to Treas. Reg. § 1.168(k)-2(g)(9), Treas. Reg. § 1.47-7(c) defines the rehabilitation credit determined as the amount equal to 20 percent of the remaining rehabilitated basis, as defined in Treas. Reg. § 1.168(k)-2(g)(9)(i)(B), of the qualified rehabilitated building for the taxable year in which such building is placed in service. Treas. Reg. § 1.47-7(c) clarifies that the Historic Tax Credit is determined in the year the qualified rehabilitated building is placed in service and allocated ratably over the five-year period under Treas. Reg. § 1.47-7(b).

As the IRS notes in the 2020 treasury regulations, the TCJA made no change to the recapture rules in Code § 50, and nothing in the legislative history of the TCJA suggests that any change to such rules was intended.[4] Accordingly, the 2020 treasury regulations incorporate the existing recapture provisions and illustrate how they work in conjunction with the ratable share rules. The 2020 treasury regulations also address the impact of the new rules on the basis adjustment provisions in Code §§ 50(c) and 50(d). A series of examples summarized next in Section 10.2.3 illustrate the IRS view of how the new rules work.

10.2.3 Examples

10.2.3.1 Example One: Historic Tax Credit Determined and Ratable Share

Between February 1, 2023, and October 1, 2023, X, a calendar year C corporation, incurred QREs of $200,000 with respect to a qualified rehabilitated building. X placed the building in service on October 15, 2023. X's Historic Tax Credit determined in 2023 is $40,000 ($200,000 × 0.20). For purposes of determining X's

4 Conference Report, at 435–36; Bluebook, at 210.

investment credit under Code § 46, for each taxable year during the five-year period beginning in 2023, the ratable share allocated for the year is $8,000 ($40,000 × 0.20).

10.2.3.2 Example Two: Coordination with Code § 50(c)

The facts are the same as in Example One. For purposes of determining the amount of X's basis adjustment in 2023 under Code § 50(c), the amount of the Historic Tax Credit is $40,000.

10.2.3.3 Example Three: Coordination with Code § 50(a)

The facts are the same as in Example One. In 2023 and 2024, X claimed the full amount of the ratable share allowed under Code § 46, or $8,000 per taxable year. X's total allowable ratable share for 2025 through 2027 is $24,000 ($8,000 allowable each taxable year). On November 1, 2025, X disposed of the qualified rehabilitated building. Under Code § 50(a)(1)(B)(iii), because the period of time between when the qualified rehabilitated building was placed in service and when it is disposed of is more than two but less than three full years, the applicable recapture percentage is 60 percent. Based on these facts, X has an increase in tax of $9,600 under Code § 50(a) ($16,000 of credit claimed in 2023 and 2024 × 0.60) and has $3,200 of credits remaining in each of 2025 through 2027, after foregoing $4,800 in credits in each of the years 2025 through 2027 ($8,000 × 0.60).

10.2.3.4 Example Four: Coordination with Code § 50(d)(5) and Treas. Reg. § 1.50-1; C Corporation Lessee

X, a calendar year C corporation, leases nonresidential real property from Y. The property is a qualified rehabilitated building that is placed in service on October 15, 2023. The amount of the Historic Tax Credit determined is $100,000. Y elects under Treas. Reg. § 1.48-4 to treat X as having acquired the property. The shortest recovery period that could be available to the property under Code § 168 is 39 years. Because Y has elected to treat X as having acquired the property, Y does not reduce its basis in the property under Code § 50(c). Instead, pursuant to Code § 50(d)(5) and Treas. Reg. § 1.50-1, X, the lessee of the property, must include ratably in gross income over 39 years an amount equal to the Historic Tax Credit determined with respect to such property.

10.2.3.5 Example Five: Coordination with Code § 50(d)(5) and Treas. Reg. § 1.50-1; Partnership Lessee

A and B, calendar year taxpayers, form a partnership, the AB partnership, that leases nonresidential real property from Y. The property is a qualified rehabilitation building that is placed in service on October 15, 2023. The amount of the Historic Tax Credit determined is $200,000. Y elects under Treas. Reg. § 1.48-4 to treat the AB partnership as having acquired the property. The shortest recovery period that could be available to the property under Code § 168 is 39 years. Because Y has elected to treat the AB partnership as having acquired the property, Y does not reduce its basis in the building under Code § 50(c). Instead, A and B, the ultimate credit claimants, as defined in Treas. Reg. § 1.50-(b)(3)(ii), must include the amount of the Historic Tax Credit with respect to A and B ratably in gross income over 39 years, the shortest recovery period available with respect to such property.

Chapter Eleven

How Do the At-Risk Rules Affect Historic Tax Credit Investments?

11.1 OVERVIEW

The ability of an investor to utilize Historic Tax Credits and losses allocated to it in a syndicated transaction also could be affected by the at-risk rules set forth in Code §§ 49 and 465.

Code § 465 contains rules that limit the deduction of losses to amounts that the taxpayer has "at risk" in an activity. Subject to certain exceptions, the provisions of Code § 465 apply to each activity engaged in by a taxpayer in connection with carrying on a trade or business or for the production of income. The Code § 465 at-risk rules apply to individuals and closely held C corporations (i.e., corporations in which, at any time during the last half of the taxable year, more than 50 percent in value of the corporation's outstanding stock is owned by five or fewer individuals).[1] Although not explicitly covered by the statutory language, estates and trusts also appear to be subject to the at-risk rules.[2] The at-risk rules do not apply to S corporations, partnerships, or LLCs (that are taxed as partnerships) as separate entities; instead, the rules apply to the shareholders, partners, and members individually. As a result, the rules could affect one or more investors in such an entity without having an impact on the remaining investors.[3]

While most investors in large syndicated Historic Tax Credit transactions are widely held corporations that are not subject to the at-risk rules, many smaller

1 I.R.C. § 465(a)(1). As a technical matter, a closely held corporation is defined as "a C corporation with respect to which the stock ownership requirement of paragraph (2) of section 542(a) is met." For purposes of this test, the I.R.C. provides that I.R.C. § 544(a)(2) shall be applied as if such section did not contain the phrase "or by or for his partner," and I.R.C. §§ 544(a)(4)(A) and 544(b)(1) shall be applied by substituting "the corporation meets the stock ownership requirements of I.R.C. § 542(a)(2)" for "the corporation is a personal holding company." It is important to note that, for purposes of determining whether the stock ownership requirements are met, Code § 542(a)(2) provides that "an organization described in section 401(a), 501(c)(17), or 509(a) or a portion of a trust permanently set aside or to be used exclusively for the purposes described in section 642(c) or a corresponding provision of a prior income tax law shall be considered an individual." For example, a blocker entity formed and controlled by a private foundation would satisfy the stock ownership test.

2 Joint Comm. on Tax'n, General Explanation of the Revenue Act of 1978, 95th Cong., 2d Sess. 134 (1979); *see also* instructions for 1995 Form 1041.

3 I.R.C. § 465(a).

projects involve individuals or closely held corporations to whom the rules do apply. Moreover, many large rehabilitation projects are structured as master lease transactions involving an election to pass the Historic Tax Credit through to a lessee partnership under Code § 50(d) and Treas. Reg. § 1.48-4. As discussed next, the credit at-risk rules may apply under such circumstances even if an investor in such lessee partnership is not directly subject to the rules.

If the provisions of Code § 465 apply, any loss from the activity for the taxable year is allowed only to the extent of the aggregate amount for which the taxpayer is at risk as of the close of the taxable year. Any excess amount is disallowed as a deduction in the current taxable year but carries forward and will be treated as a deduction allocable to the activity in the first succeeding taxable years. Disallowed losses also may be deducted in a later taxable year to the extent of any gain recognized upon disposition of the activity.

In general, a taxpayer is treated as being at risk to the extent of (i) the amount of money and the adjusted basis of other property contributed by the taxpayer to a specified activity and (ii) certain amounts borrowed by the taxpayer for use in such activity.

11.2 CREDIT AT-RISK RULES

11.2.1 Overview

Taxpayers described in Code § 465(a)(1) are subject to a separate set of at-risk rules in Code § 49 that apply to property based tax credits such as the Historic Tax Credit. Under those rules, the "credit base" of investment credit property (including property that is eligible for the Historic Tax Credit) must be reduced by the "nonqualified nonrecourse financing" with respect to such credit base (determined as of the close of the taxable year in which the property is placed in service). For this purpose, the credit base includes, among other things, "the portion of the basis of any qualified rehabilitated building attributable to qualified rehabilitation expenditures."[4]

11.2.2 Nonqualified Nonrecourse Financing

Nonqualified nonrecourse financing means any nonrecourse financing that is not "qualified commercial financing." Qualified commercial financing is defined as any financing (other than convertible debt) with respect to any property if:

(i) such property is acquired by the taxpayer from a person who is not a related person;
(ii) the amount of the nonrecourse financing with respect to such property does not exceed 80 percent of the credit base of such property; and

4 *Id.* § 49(a)(1)(C)(i).

(iii) such financing is borrowed from a qualified person or represents a loan from any federal, state, or local government or instrumentality thereof, or is guaranteed by any federal, state, or local government.[5]

For purposes of this rule, a "qualified person" is a person who, among other things, is actively and regularly engaged in the business of lending money. In addition, a qualified person may not be (i) a related person with respect to the taxpayer, (ii) a person from whom the taxpayer acquired the property (or a related person to such person), or (iii) a person who receives a fee with respect to the taxpayer's investment in the property (or a related person to such person).[6] The Code provides that in the case of a partnership or an S corporation, the determination of whether a partner's or shareholder's allocable share of any financing is nonqualified nonrecourse financing shall be made at the partner or shareholder level and that such determination shall be made in the same manner as the "credit allowable by section 38 with respect to such property."[7]

For purposes of applying the credit at-risk rules, nonrecourse financing includes:

(i) any amount with respect to which the taxpayer is protected against loss through guarantees, stop-loss agreements, or other similar arrangements, and

(ii) except to the extent provided in regulations, any amount borrowed from a person who has an interest (other than as a creditor) in the activity in which the property is used or from a related person to a person (other than the taxpayer) having such an interest.[8]

It is important to note that a loan that purports to be a recourse obligation may be deemed to be nonrecourse if such loan falls within either of these two categories.

For purposes of applying these rules, the term "related person" has the same meaning as is set forth in Code § 465(b)(3)(C). Under this provision, a person (referred to herein as the "related person") is related to any person if (i) the related person bears a relationship to such person specified in Code § 267(b) or Code § 707(b)(1), or (ii) the related person and such person are engaged in trades or business under common control (within the meaning of subsections (a) and (b) of Code § 52). For purposes of applying clause (i), the references to "50 percent" in Code §§ 267(b) and 707(b)(1) are replaced with references to "10 percent."

5 *Id.* § 49(a)(1)(D)(ii).
6 *Id.* § 49(a)(1)(D)(iv).
7 *Id.* § 49(a)(1)(E)(i), (a)(1)(F).
8 *Id.* § 49(a)(1)(D)(iii).

As noted earlier, the Code provides that the investment tax credit at-risk rules apply to any property that is placed in service during the taxable year by a taxpayer described in Code § 465(a)(1) (i.e., an individual or closely held C corporation) and is used in connection with an activity for which any loss is subject to limitation under Code § 465.[9]

11.3 HOW DO THE CREDIT AT-RISK RULES APPLY TO CODE § 50(d) LEASE PASS-THROUGH TRANSACTIONS?

Under Former Code § 48(d), a lessor of investment credit property who made an election to pass the investment tax credit relating to the property to a lessee was subject to the at-risk rules contained in Former Code § 46(c)(8) and now set forth in Code § 49(a). Based on the language of Code § 50(d)(5), similar at-risk rules presumably will apply in the case of an election under Code § 50(d). Under these rules, if the at-risk rules apply to the lessor, the lessee's credit will be limited to the amount of credit that would have been available to the lessor if the lessor's basis in the property was equal to the lessee's acquisition amount and the lessor had not made an election to treat the lessee as the purchaser of the property.

Former Code § 48(d)(6)(B) also provided that certain lessees in transactions involving an election under Former Code § 48(d) would be subject to the at-risk rules. An "at-risk lessee" was defined as any lessee who is a taxpayer subject to at-risk rules set forth in Code § 465(a)(1). These rules apply to "at-risk property," which is defined as any property used by an at-risk lessee in connection with an activity that is subject to the at-risk rules set forth in Code § 465.

In order to avoid a reduction in the amount of any investment tax credit passed through to it under Former Code § 48(d), an at-risk lessee was required to have a minimum at-risk percentage. This percentage was determined by dividing the present value (discounted on the basis of the underpayment rate established in Code § 6621 in effect at the time of the execution of the lease) of the aggregate "lease at-risk payments" by the so-called "lessee acquisition amount." The "lessee acquisition amount" was defined as the amount for which the lessee was treated as having acquired the property for by reason of the credit pass-through election. To avoid a reduction in the available credit, the at-risk percentage of the lessee had to exceed the sum of (i) two times the sum of the credit percentages applicable to the property under Former Code § 46(a) plus (ii) 10 percent. The "at-risk percentage" was the percentage obtained by dividing (i) the present value (determined as of the time the lease was entered into) of the aggregate lease at-risk payments by (ii) the lessee acquisition amount. The term "lease at-risk payment" was defined to mean any rental payment (i) that the lessee was required to make under the lease in all events and (ii) with respect to

9 *Id.* § 49(a)(1)(B).

which the lessee was not protected against loss through nonrecourse financing, guarantees, stop-loss agreements, or other similar arrangements.[10]

Assuming that the investor in a lessee entity involving a Code § 50(d)(5) election is not subject to the at-risk rules, it will not be characterized as an "at-risk lessee." However, the at-risk rules still could apply to a transaction in which such investor invests in the lessee, and the lessor (or its partners or members) are subject to the at-risk rules.

With respect to the lessor, Former Code § 48(b)(6)(A) provided that if (i) a lessor made an election to pass through the credit with respect to any at-risk property leased to an at-risk lessee, and (ii) but for the provisions of Former Code § 48(b)(6)(A), the at-risk provisions of Former Code § 46(c)(8) (currently Code § 49(a)) would not apply to such property in the hands of the lessor, Former Code § 46(c)(8) (currently Code § 49(a)) would apply to the lessor with respect to such property unless (i) the lessor manufactured or produced the property, (ii) the property had a readily ascertainable fair market value, or (iii) in circumstances determined by the Secretary of the Treasury to be circumstances where the application of this rule was not necessary to carry out the purposes of Former Code § 46(c)(8) (currently Code § 49(a)).

Moreover, in the case of any property that, in the hands of the lessor, was property to which Former Code § 46(c)(8) (currently Code § 49(a)) applied, the amount of the credit allowable to the lessee in the event of an election under Former Code § 48(d) with respect to such property could at no time exceed the credit that would have been allowable to the lessor with respect to such property (determined without regard to Former Code § 46(e)(3)) if (i) the lessor's basis in such property was equal to the lessee's acquisition amount and (ii) no election had been made to treat the lessee as the purchaser of the property under Former Code § 48(d). In other words, even if no at-risk lessee is involved, to the extent that the lessor (or the lessor's partners or members) are subject to the at-risk rules, the lessor cannot pass through to the lessee a larger credit than the lessor (or its partners or members) could have taken if the election was not made.

11.4 HOW TO ANALYZE THE IMPACT OF THE AT-RISK RULES

In determining the impact of the at-risk rules on a transaction, the initial issue is whether the taxpayers involved are subject to such rules. As noted previously, in the case of a partnership, the credit at-risk provisions are applied at the partner level. As a result, in order to apply the at-risk rules, it is necessary to determine which members of the owner are subject to such rules and to quantify their respective shares of the financing in question. In the case of a member that is itself a pass-through entity, the analysis must extend to the ultimate partners or members of such entity.

10 *Id.* § 48(d)(6)(C)(v) *repealed by* Pub. L. No. 101-508, 104 Stat. 1388-1, 536–59 (1990).

If at-risk taxpayers are involved, it is necessary to determine which liabilities of the owner will be deemed to constitute "financing" with respect to the "property" (i.e., the improvements funded with the QREs incurred in connection with the rehabilitation) for purposes of the at-risk rules. Once the amount of the financing has been determined, the next question is how much of such financing will be deemed to be "nonrecourse" for purposes of the at-risk rules. Under such rules, up to 80 percent of the cost of the rehabilitation may be financed on a nonrecourse basis provided that the person providing the financing is a qualified person.

The term "nonrecourse" generally means a lack of personal liability on the part of the borrower. It also means any amount with respect to which the taxpayer is protected against loss through a stop-loss agreement, guarantee, or other protection. Finally, nonrecourse debt includes any amount borrowed from a person having an interest (other than as a creditor) in the activity for which the property is used or from a related person to a person other than the taxpayer with such an interest. However, recourse borrowing by the taxpayer from a related person is not treated as nonrecourse by reason of the taxpayer's interest in the activity. In addition, recourse borrowing by a corporation from a shareholder will not be treated as nonrecourse financing for this purpose.

Financing for the rehabilitation of an historic building often is provided from multiple sources, including both debt and equity. In many cases, there may be more than one loan, in which event each loan must be analyzed to determine whether it constitutes nonqualified nonrecourse financing, thereby mandating a reduction in the credit base created by the QREs incurred in connection with the rehabilitation. Since the proceeds of the loans (as well as other sources of funds) typically are applied to pay a wide variety of expenditures in addition to QREs, the initial question is how to determine the amount of nonrecourse financing "with respect to" the credit base. This determination is necessary in order to apply the 80 percent test described previously. Although no definitive authority exists with respect to this issue, the IRS has addressed the issue in various private letter rulings. In a 1988 private letter ruling, the IRS considered a rehabilitation project that was financed by two nonrecourse loans that met the first, third, and fourth test for "qualified commercial financing" described earlier, and by equity contributions from the partners.[11] In applying the 80 percent test, and without citing any specific authority, the IRS permitted a pro rata allocation of the debt across all the project costs and held that the nonrecourse financing for the project satisfied the requirements under Former Code § 46(c)(8) and would not mandate a reduction in the credit base because neither (i) the pro rata allocation of nonrecourse financing nor (ii) each partner's pro rata share of such nonrecourse financing exceeded 80 percent of the credit base.

11 Priv. Ltr. Rul. 8828063 (Apr. 18, 1988).

Subsequently, in a 1990 private letter ruling, the IRS again confirmed its support for the pro rata allocation method.[12] In this transaction, the partnership made representations to the IRS concerning the expected costs of the rehabilitation, the costs of purchasing the interest of the old lessees and entering into new leases, the amount of operating deficit expenses, and the fair market value of the building before the rehabilitation. Financing fees were allocated across the other expenses and the value of the building based on their relative costs (or value). The partnership determined the amount of its nonrecourse debt "with respect to" the rehabilitation expenditures by dividing the cost of the rehabilitation expenditures by the sum of the foregoing amounts and multiplying this fraction by the amount of the nonrecourse debt. The IRS ruled that this allocation method was reasonable and resulted in no reduction of the credit base. In determining what portion of the loan was incurred with respect to the rehabilitation, the IRS concluded that the loan should be allocated among the existing building, the rehabilitation costs, the buyout of the leases, and the rent-up expenses based on the fair market value of the building on the date that the loan was secured and on the costs of the rehabilitation work, the buyout of the leases, and such rent-up expenses.[13]

Assuming the pro rata approach applies, the initial step in the 80 percent analysis is to determine the percentage that the QREs incurred in connection with the rehabilitation bears to the total project costs. This percentage is then applied to the nonrecourse debt of the owner to determine the amount of such debt incurred with respect to the credit base.

As should be evident from the foregoing discussion, the credit at-risk rules in Code § 49 are extremely complicated and difficult to apply, and there is very little administrative or judicial authority dealing with these rules. A series of examples will serve to illustrate some of the complexities and lack of clarity that exist in this area.[14]

11.4.1 Example One

P, a general partnership comprised of equal partners A and B, borrows $100,000 from A's wife in connection with an historic rehabilitation project. No credit pass-through election will be made under Code § 50(d). For state law purposes, both A and B are personally liable for the repayment of the loan. It appears that, in the case of A, this loan is not nonrecourse financing since the amount is being borrowed from a related person to A, who is the taxpayer as to whom the

12 Priv. Ltr. Rul. 9004005 (Oct. 16, 1989).

13 *See also* Priv. Ltr. Rul. 9016032 (Jan. 19, 1990).

14 The following examples are based in part on examples from John Hanlee, Jr., *At-Risk Rules*, BNA Tax Management Portfolio 455, § XIIIB (2d ed.) (1996).

determination is being made. However, if P borrowed the same amount directly from A, the statutory language would appear to characterize A's share of the loan as nonrecourse, since A has a direct interest as a partner in the activity. This does not seem to make much sense. From a policy perspective, it is difficult to understand why A's share of the credit base should be reduced if he loans money to the venture but not if his wife makes the loan or he contributes the funds as equity. Note that the loan from A's wife would be nonrecourse as to B since it was made by a related person to a person (other than the partner for whom the determination is being made) who has an interest in the activity.

11.4.2 Example Two

A and B are equal partners in general partnership P. A owns 20 percent of the stock of C Corporation. If C loans money to P to finance the rehabilitation, the loan is recourse as to A but is nonrecourse as to B, since C is related to A, who has an interest in the activity. On the other hand, if A loans money to P to finance the rehabilitation, the loan will be treated as nonrecourse as to both A and B, since Code § 49(a)(1)(D)(iii)(II) provides that a loan borrowed from a person who has an interest (other than as a creditor) in the activity is treated as nonrecourse.

11.4.3 Example Three

A limited partnership intends to rehabilitate an existing building that constitutes a certified historic structure. A is the GP with a 5 percent interest in the partnership and B is the investor with a 95 percent interest. Assume further that a deferred developer fee is owed by the partnership to the developer, which is an entity is related to A. In his capacity as general partner, A is personally liable for the payment of the deferred fee. As a result, he would not appear to be "protected against loss" within the meaning of Code § 49(a)(1)(D)(iii). The issue, therefore, becomes whether the fee is "borrowed from a person who has an interest (other than as a creditor) in the activity in which the property is used or from a related person to a person (other than the taxpayer) having such an interest."

The developer does not have an interest in the activity, but is related to a person (i.e., A) who does have such an interest. However, the parenthetical reference to a person "(other than the taxpayer)" should result in a determination that the deferred fee will not be deemed to be nonrecourse financing as to A.

The analysis with respect to B is different. The developer is not related to B. Moreover, as a limited partner, B has no personal liability for the payment of the deferred developer fee. Therefore, as to B, the deferred fee is "borrowed" from a related person to a person (i.e., the developer is related to A) having an interest in the activity. Since the developer is not related to B, who is the taxpayer to whom the test is being applied, the parenthetical "(other than the taxpayer)" does not apply and, as to B, the deferred fee *will* constitute nonrecourse financing.

Assuming that the developer is not a qualified person, this means that 95 percent of the deferred fee would constitute nonqualified, nonrecourse financing, resulting in a reduction in the credit base under the provisions of Code § 49(a). The Historic Tax Credit is based on 20 percent of the QREs (i.e., the credit base). Accordingly, there would be a deferral of 19 percent (i.e., 95 percent of 20 percent) of the Historic Tax Credit that otherwise would be allocable to B. When the fee ultimately is paid, there would be an increase in the credit base and a resulting credit allowed to B.

What if the partnership elected to pass the Historic Tax Credit arising from the rehabilitation of the building through to D, the master tenant under the terms of a qualified lease and the provisions of Code § 50(d)? In this example, the "lender" is the developer. The developer is related to A, but A has a 10 percent or less interest in P. Accordingly, the developer is not related to the partnership. However, since the developer is not regularly engaged in the lending of money, the deferred developer fee does not constitute qualified commercial financing as to the partnership. As a result, the credit base passed through to D must be reduced by the entire amount of the deferred fee. If the developer, in its capacity as a real estate developer, regularly receives deferred fees for its development services, query whether the parties could argue that the developer is regularly engaged in the lending of money. Would the developer then be a "qualified person"? Could the IRS argue that the deferred developer fee is "a fee with respect to the taxpayer's investment in the property"? At present, there are no definitive answers to these questions.

11.4.4 Example Four

A limited partnership comprised of A and B as equal general and limited partners rehabilitates a commercial office building that constitutes a certified historic structure. An investor, C, who is subject to the at-risk rules, contributes substantial equity to the partnership in return for a 99 percent limited partnership interest in operating profits and losses and a 20 percent interest in sale or refinancing proceeds. Following the admission of C to the partnership, A and B each retains a 0.5 percent interest as a general partner in operating profits and losses and a 40 percent interest in sale or refinancing proceeds. As part of the development costs, the partnership agrees to pay a deferred developer fee of $1 million to the developer, which is an LLC in which A and B each own a 50 percent interest as members.

Assuming the deferred fee is treated as financing, the question is whether A is at risk for any portion of such fee. Here, the "borrower" is the partnership (but for this purpose A, since the analysis is applied at the partner level) and the "lender" is the developer. The amount is borrowed from the developer, which does not have an interest in the activity (i.e., the rehabilitation). However, under

Code § 707(b)(1), as modified for at-risk purposes, a partnership and a person owning more than 10 percent of the capital or profits interests are related. As a result, both A and B are related to the developer (assuming the developer is treated as a partnership for federal income tax purposes).

Applying the preceding rules to A, the deferred fee is borrowed from a related person to a person (other than A, the taxpayer) having an interest in the activity. In other words, the developer is related to B, who has an interest in the activity. The fact that the developer also is related to A does not appear to matter even though, considered separately, that relationship would prevent the deferred fee from being treated as nonrecourse financing because of the "(other than the taxpayer)" caveat. Accordingly, as to A, the deferred fee would constitute nonrecourse financing (and presumably nonqualified nonrecourse financing).

The foregoing analysis would appear to mandate the same result for B.

What about C? The fee is borrowed from a related person to a person (other than C, the taxpayer) having an interest in the activity. Again, the fee would appear to constitute nonrecourse financing (and presumably nonqualified nonrecourse financing) as to C.

It could be argued that, at least in the context of a deferred fee, this result is justified from a policy perspective since it prevents taxpayers from artificially increasing the credit base of a rehabilitated building by paying an inflated fee to themselves. On the other hand, one might well ask why a taxpayer would agree to pay income tax on a fee at a significant combined federal and state tax rate in return for the equity that could be raised by including the fee in the credit base. If one assumes that C has agreed to contribute to capital $0.90 for each $1.00 of Historic Tax Credit allocated to it, the maximum benefit to A and B, the taxpayer developers, would be 90 percent of 20 percent (the amount of the Historic Tax Credit), or 18 percent of the amount of the fee. On the other hand, A and B may be required to pay substantial federal, state, and local income taxes upon receipt of the fee. Unless the payment of the fee is to be deferred for a long period or A and B have losses that can be applied against the income, the trade does not seem to make much sense.

11.4.5 Example Five

Assume A and B form a limited partnership in which A is the GP with a 5 percent interest and B is the limited partner with a 95 percent interest. B's interest will be reduced to 85 percent when T, a limited liability company, is admitted to the partnership as described next. The partnership acquires a building that qualifies as a certified historic structure and intends to rehabilitate it in a manner that will qualify for the Historic Tax Credit. The seller of the building is unrelated to A, B, or T. Upon completion of the rehabilitation, the partnership intends to master lease the building to T, who will operate it as a commercial office building and sublease it to unrelated commercial tenants. The Historic Tax Credit arising from the rehabilitation will be passed through by the partnership to T pursuant to the terms of Code § 50(d). The total cost of the rehabilitation is expected to be $12 million, of which $8 million is expected to qualify as QREs, producing an Historic Tax Credit of $1,600,000. Included in such QREs is a development fee to the developer in the amount of $1,200,000, of which $1,000,000 will be deferred and paid from cash available to the partnership from rent and other sources during the five years following completion of the rehabilitation. The developer is related to A but not to B. Construction financing in the amount of $7,200,000 is being provided by an unrelated institutional lender. The construction loan is a recourse obligation of the partnership for which A, as the GP, bears the economic risk of loss. A has contributed no capital to the partnership. B has contributed $2 million to the capital of the partnership.

T has received a commitment from an equity investor that is a public company to contribute $1,440,000 to the capital of T in return for certain economic benefits and 99 percent of the Historic Tax Credit passed through by the partnership to T. The partnership has received a commitment for permanent financing in the amount of $7,200,000 from another unrelated institutional lender. The permanent loan will be nonrecourse to the partnership and its partners.

T has agreed to acquire a 10 percent limited partnership interest in the partnership in exchange for a capital contribution of $1 million. T's capital contribution to the partnership will be funded over a period of approximately two years using a portion of the capital contributions made by the investor to T.

The deferred developer fee owed to the developer is a recourse obligation of the partnership (and, therefore, A in its capacity as GP) and does not bear interest.

How will the at-risk rules affect the amount of the Historic Tax Credit that can be passed through to T? The threshold issue is to determine the amount of nonrecourse financing with respect to the credit base. The construction loan is recourse as to A but nonrecourse as to both B and T. Assume that neither the investor nor the managing member of T is subject to the at-risk rules. The construction loan will qualify as qualified commercial financing if the total nonrecourse financing with respect to the property does not exceed 80 percent of the credit base, and the other conditions set forth in Code § 49(a)(1)(D) are satisfied. Since the total credit base in this example is $8 million, the maximum nonrecourse debt is $6,400,000. The credit base of $8 million is 66 2/3 percent of the total project cost of $12 million. If the same two-thirds ratio is applied to the sum of the construction loan and the deferred developer fee ($8,200,000), the resulting amount is $5,466,666, which is less than the maximum allowable amount of $6,400,000. Accordingly, the 80 percent test should be satisfied. Moreover, since the property was not acquired from a related person to any of the partnership's partners and the construction lender is regularly engaged in the business of lending money, the construction loan should constitute qualified commercial financing even though it is nonrecourse financing with respect to B and T.

A similar analysis must be undertaken with respect to the deferred developer fee. Assume that the development agreement between the partnership and the developer provides that the deferred developer fee will be paid from cash available to the partnership from rent paid by T under the master lease and the capital contributions from T to the partnership. If the deferred developer fee has not been fully paid by the partnership to the developer within five years following completion of the rehabilitation, A is required to contribute to the partnership an amount sufficient to enable P to pay the unpaid amount of the deferred developer fee to the developer. As noted earlier, the developer is related to A but not to B. However, since A has a less than 10 percent interest in the partnership, the developer will not be deemed to be related to the partnership. As to A, the deferred developer fee arguably is recourse rather than nonrecourse financing since the ultimate responsibility for the payment of the fee rests with A, and the fee is not payable to a related person to a person "other than the taxpayer" (i.e., A) with an interest in the activity. In the case of B and T, however, the deferred developer fee would be considered to be nonrecourse financing since B and T, as the limited partners of the partnership, have no liability to pay the fee. Since the members of T are not subject to the at-risk rules, the fact that the fee is nonrecourse financing to T (and its members) should be irrelevant.

The next issue to be considered is whether the deferred developer fee would be "nonqualified" nonrecourse financing by virtue of its failure to satisfy the conditions set forth in the definition of qualified commercial financing. The first condition is that the property cannot have been acquired by the taxpayer from a related person. That is not an issue here. The second condition is that the nonrecourse financing "with respect to" the property does not exceed 80 percent of the credit base of such property. As already described, the 80 percent test should be satisfied in this example. However, unless the developer can be said to be regularly engaged in the lending business as a result of a recurring practice of accepting deferred fees for its development services, the deferred developer fee cannot constitute qualified commercial financing. As a result, for purposes of determining the amount of the Historic Tax Credit that can be passed through to T, it is likely that the credit base will have to be reduced by a portion of the deferred developer fee until such fee is actually paid. Presumably, this portion would be B's 85 percent share of the $1 million deferred developer fee, or $850,000. This would result in a deferral of $170,000 of the Historic Tax Credit passed through to T pursuant to the terms of the master lease (20 percent of $850,000).

If no Code § 50(d) election were involved, the likely result would be that, in the case of A, no reduction in A's share of the credit base would be required, since both the construction loan and the deferred developer fee would be deemed to be recourse debt. As to B, however, both the construction loan and the deferred developer fee would be nonrecourse. Since the construction loan constitutes qualified commercial financing, there should be no reduction in B's share of the credit base in the case of such financing. The deferred developer fee, however, presumably would constitute nonqualified nonrecourse financing as to B, and B's share of the credit base would be reduced by the amount of such fee until it is paid.

Chapter Twelve

Tax Structuring Issues

Historic Boardwalk Hall and Other Challenges to Historic Tax Credit Transactions

12.1 BACKGROUND

The Historic Tax Credit was first enacted (in a slightly different form) in 1978. During the early years after its enactment, most syndicated Historic Tax Credit transactions involved the direct admission of a group of high net worth individuals as limited partners of the partnership that owned the building(s) that were the subject of the rehabilitation. An affiliate of the developer typically would serve as the general partner. The limited partners would be allocated substantially all (usually 99 percent) of the partnership's "bottom line" profits and Historic Tax Credits. The developer/general partner would retain the lion's share of the economic benefits through a combination of development, property management, and incentive management fees; priority cash distributions; and/or "flip" structures in which the limited partners' shares of profits and losses would "flip" down after the five-year recapture period.

Following the passage of the Tax Reform Act of 1986, the passive activity rules in Code § 469 significantly reduced the ability of individuals and closely held corporations to utilize Historic Tax Credits and other similar tax benefits. Although some public funds catering to individual investors remained, the Historic Tax Credit equity market gradually became largely the domain of large corporate and institutional investors that were not subject to the passive activity rules. Moreover, for the reasons discussed in Section 9.2, by the early 2000s, the structure of choice for syndicated Historic Tax Credit transactions became the use of a master lease with an election under Code § 50(d) (and Treas. Reg. § 1.48-4) to pass the credit through to the lessee/master tenant (or its partners or members).[1]

12.2 MASTER LEASE STRUCTURE

Under the original master lease approach, the developer/owner of the historic building(s) would undertake the rehabilitation using its own funds, together with mortgage proceeds, state and local subsidies, and sometimes equity from

1 *See* Section 9.2.

economic investors. Upon completion of the rehabilitation, the building(s) would be leased to a master tenant entity (usually a limited partnership or LLC) that would sublease the completed project to the actual users, which could include commercial or residential tenants, a hotel or theatre operator, or similar end users. In some cases, the building(s) would be leased back to an affiliate of the owner/landlord, who then would operate the property. The general partner or managing member of the master tenant would be an affiliate of the owner/landlord. The owner/landlord then would make an election under Code § 50(d) (and Treas. Reg. § 1.48-4) to pass the Historic Tax Credit arising from the rehabilitation through to the master tenant. The Historic Tax Credit equity investor would be admitted to the master tenant as a limited partner or investor member and would contribute equity to the master tenant in exchange for an allocation of substantially all (typically between 99 percent and 99.99 percent) of the "bottom line" profits and Historic Tax Credits passed through by the owner/landlord, as well as a negotiated share of the cash flow generated at the master tenant level.

The capital contributed to the master tenant by the investor would then be applied to one or more of the following: (i) the acquisition by the master tenant of an equity interest in the owner/landlord, (ii) the payment of prepaid rent to the owner/landlord (which would be subject to the provisions of Code § 467), (iii) the acquisition of furniture, fixtures, and equipment or other non-credit eligible property required by the master tenant to conduct its operations, or (iv) a loan to the owner/landlord.

In most cases, at the end of the five-year recapture period, the investor would have a put option to require the general partner or managing member of the master tenant to purchase its interest (usually for a nominal amount). If the put option were not exercised, the general partner/managing member would have a call option to purchase the investor's interest for an amount equal to its fair market value (which often was not significant because of the lease terms, lack of control and marketability, and similar factors). As discussed in Section 9.2, the master tenant would treat the so-called "section 50(d) income" as a partnership item for tax purposes that would increase the tax basis (and Code § 704(b) capital account) of the investor and thus decrease any gain (or increase any capital loss) on the sale of the investor's interest.

12.3 JUDICIAL AND ADMINISTRATIVE EFFORTS TO COMBAT CORPORATE TAX SHELTERS

12.3.1 Overview

During the period in which more sophisticated structures for monetizing the Historic Tax Credit evolved, both Congress and the IRS were turning their attention to the proliferation of corporate tax shelter transactions cutting across multiple industries. In particular, the IRS began to express significant concerns about what it viewed as the inappropriate use of complicated partnership and multiparty leasing structures to avoid taxes. It became apparent to the IRS, Congress, and the courts that existing restrictions on tax shelters—such as the passive activity and at-risk rules—were not sufficient to address all of the perceived abuses. Congress and the IRS responded to the situation by enacting or promulgating a series of new structuring provisions, rules, and regulations to combat the increasingly intricate structured transactions being developed by the large law and accounting firms, including the enactment of the reportable and listed transaction rules, the publication of the partnership anti-abuse regulations under Code § 701, the enactment of increased penalties for tax shelter transactions, restrictions on the participation by tax-exempt organizations in such transactions, the adoption of significant amendments to Treasury Circular 230, the eventual codification of the economic substance doctrine in Code § 7701(o), and various other measures.

At the same time, the courts began to turn to a lethal arsenal of common law judicial doctrines in analyzing tax shelter transactions, including the economic substance, substance over form, step transaction, and sham transaction doctrines. No clear line of demarcation exists between many of these doctrines, which often were conflated by the courts in reaching what they viewed to be an appropriate result. Of overriding importance to participants in syndicated Historic Tax Credit transactions were two issues: (i) how would the economic substance doctrine be applied to tax credits enacted to incentivize investments in socially beneficial areas, and (ii) when will a purported partnership be recognized as such for federal income tax purposes? Both of these issues are discussed next.

12.3.2 The Economic Substance Doctrine

The first issue was the vexing question of how to apply the economic substance doctrine to transactions involving so-called "targeted" tax credits (such as the Historic Tax Credit) that were enacted by Congress to incentivize investments in socially desirable areas.

Many historic rehabilitation projects, particularly theatres and other community development projects and affordable housing developments, generate relatively modest amounts of pre-tax cash flow. It can be persuasively argued that one of the main reasons Congress enacted the Historic Tax Credit, and other targeted tax credits such as energy credits, low-income housing tax credits, and new markets tax credits, was to create an incentive for socially beneficial investments notwithstanding the absence of a traditional cash-on-cash return.

Such targeted tax credit investments, however, often run afoul of the traditional conjunctive multifactor economic substance analysis developed by the courts and now codified in Code § 7701(o) under which tax benefits from an investment can be denied unless the taxpayer can demonstrate *both* a business purpose for, and a reasonable expectation of a pre-tax profit from, the investment.

A crucial issue in the economic substance analysis has become whether, in applying the economic substance doctrine in leasing and other tax-oriented transactions, targeted tax credits may be treated as the equivalent of cash.[2]

In *Friendship Dairies*, the Tax Court held that a leasing transaction in which the lessor anticipated realizing a pre-tax loss of approximately $50,000 while obtaining the benefit of an investment tax credit of about $200,000 was a sham. In its opinion, the Tax Court refused to treat the credit as the equivalent of cash, reasoning that the investment tax credit generally was not intended to be a subsidy but rather was a substitute for a "capital investment deduction" that was available to all business entities. In reviewing the legislative history of the investment tax credit, the Tax Court found nothing to indicate that the credit was intended to "transform unprofitable transactions into profitable ones."

Notwithstanding the Tax Court's decision in *Friendship Dairies*, there is considerable evidence that its holding was not intended to apply to targeted tax credits that are specifically designed to incentivize investments that otherwise might not be made because of a lack of profitability or other factors.

In the oft-cited *Sacks* case, for example, the Ninth Circuit, reversing the Tax Court, held that a taxpayer was entitled to depreciation deductions and investment tax credits arising out of the sale and leaseback of solar water heating equipment, concluding that such transactions were not shams.

With respect to economic substance, the court concluded that "where a transaction has economic substance, it does not become a sham merely because it is likely to be unprofitable on a pre-tax basis." The court reasoned that the absence of pre-tax profit did not indicate "whether the transaction had economic substance where Congress has purposely used tax incentives to change [lessors'] conduct" and induce the investment in solar energy. In the view of the court, if "the government treats tax-advantaged transactions as shams unless they make economic sense on a pre-tax basis, then it takes away with the executive hand what it gives with the legislative." In effect, reasoned the court, the IRS was attempting to use the reason Congress created the tax credits as a grounds for denying them, which "would violate the principle that statutes ought to be construed in light of their purposes." If tax benefits that are specially authorized by Congress are denied to taxpayers when an investment is made because of the tax benefits, then the only investments that taxpayers would make would be investments that would have been made without this availability of the tax benefits. The court noted that the legislative intent behind the solar tax credits was to induce investments that would not otherwise have been made because

2 *See* Friendship Dairies v. Comm'r, 90 T.C. 1054 (1988); Sacks v. Comm'r, 69 F.3d 982, 95 TNT 218-13 (9th Cir. 1995); Rose v. Comm'r, 88 T.C. 386, 87 TNT 25–11 (1987), *aff'd*, 868 F.2d 851, 89 TNT 65–3 (6th Cir. 1989).

absent the tax credits the investments are not profitable. Unlike the investment tax credit in *Friendship Dairies*, Congress had purposefully skewed the neutrality of the tax system not just to vaguely "encourage" investment in the specific area of alternative energy. Instead, the energy credit qualified as a subsidy and, therefore, should be viewed as the equivalent of cash. Accordingly, the court concluded that the transaction should not be considered to be a sham transaction "just because its profitability was based on after-tax instead of pre-tax projections."[3]

In addition to the *Sacks* decision, a series of other developments suggested that a modified version of the economic substance doctrine should apply to transactions involving credits intended by Congress to incentivize investments in socially beneficial areas. For example, in 2005 the Joint Committee on Taxation issued a report concluding that most renewable energy projects would be unprofitable without the subsidy provided by production credits, in effect explicitly acknowledging that such credits should be viewed as cash in applying the economic substance doctrine.[4] Subsequently, in 2007, the IRS issued Revenue Procedure 2007-65 providing a safe harbor for allocations of production credits that appeared to support the notion that such credits could be included as the equivalent of cash in calculating an investor's expected return for purposes of applying the economic substance doctrine.[5]

In particular, Code § 7701(o) codified the economic substance doctrine, effective for transactions entered into after March 30, 2010 (the enactment date of the legislation). Code § 7701(o) generally provides that, in a case in which a court determines that the economic substance doctrine is relevant to a transaction (or a series of transactions), such transaction (or series of transactions) will be deemed to have economic substance (and thus to satisfy the economic substance doctrine) only if the taxpayer establishes that (i) the transaction changes in a meaningful way (apart from federal income tax consequences) the taxpayer's economic position, and (ii) the taxpayer has a substantial nonfederal income tax purpose for entering into such transaction.

In general, Code § 7701(o) confirms the holding of certain judicial decisions that, when applying the economic substance doctrine, there must be *both* (i) an objective inquiry concerning the effects of the transaction on the economic position of the taxpayer and (ii) a subjective inquiry concerning the taxpayer's

3 *Sacks*, 69 F.3d 982, 95 TNT 218-13.

4 Joint Committee on Tax'n, Present Law and Background Relating to the Tax Credits for Electricity Production from Renewable Sources, JCX-36-05, at 15 (May 19, 2005).

5 2007-45 I.R.B. 967. *See also* Priv. Ltr. Rul. 8911025 (Dec. 16, 1988) and Treas. Reg. § 1.42-4(a) stating that Code § 183 will not be applied to disallow losses, credits, and deductions attributable to the ownership of a building eligible for low-income housing tax credits. Interestingly, the regulatory language does provide that such benefits may be disallowed under other Code provisions or judicial doctrines, including the economic substance doctrine.

motives for engaging in the transaction. In order to be respected, the transaction must satisfy both tests. Code § 7701(o) permits a taxpayer to rely on factors other than profit potential to demonstrate that a transaction results in a meaningful change in the taxpayer's economic position or that the taxpayer has a substantial nonfederal income tax purpose for entering into such transaction. However, if a taxpayer does rely on profit potential, the present value of the reasonably expected pre-federal tax profit must be substantial compared to the present value of the expected net federal tax benefits that would be allowed if the transaction were respected. In determining pre-federal tax profits, fees and other transaction expenses (and, to the extent provided by regulations, foreign taxes) will be treated as expenses.

In a notice issued in September of 2010, the IRS stated that it would continue to rely on relevant case law under the common law economic substance doctrine in applying the two-prong conjunctive test in Code § 7701(o)(1), as well as in determining whether the present value of the reasonably expected pre-tax profit is substantial in relation to the present value of the expected net tax benefits that would be allowed if the transaction were respected for federal income tax purposes.[6] The IRS also stated that to ensure consistent administration of the strict liability penalty imposed under Code § 7701 and discussed later, any decision to impose the doctrine (and related penalty) at the examination level must be reviewed and approved by the appropriate Director of Field Operations.

In conjunction with the enactment of Code § 7701(o), Congress also introduced a strict liability penalty for violations of the codified economic substance doctrine. Under Code § 6664(c)(1), no penalty generally is imposed under either Code § 6662 (the accuracy-related penalty) or Code § 6663 (the fraud penalty) if it is shown that there was a reasonable cause for the position taken by the taxpayer and the taxpayer acted in good faith regarding the position taken. However, Code § 6662 imposes a strict liability penalty that applies whether or not the taxpayer has a reasonable basis for its position or acted in good faith. In the case of a disclosed transaction, the penalty is 20 percent of the understatement. This amount is increased to 40 percent of the understatement if the taxpayer does not adequately disclose the relevant facts affecting the tax treatment in the return or in a statement attached to the return.[7]

Unless the transaction is a "reportable transaction," the adequate disclosure requirements will be satisfied if a taxpayer adequately discloses on a timely filed original return (determined with regard to extensions) or a "qualified amended return," the relevant facts affecting the tax treatment of the transaction.[8]

6 *See* Notice 2010-62 issued on September 13, 2010; LB+I Directive, LMSB-20-0910-024.

7 I.R.C. §§ 6662(i), 6664(c)(2), 6664(d)(2), 6676(c).

8 *See* Notice 2010-62, Treas. Reg. § 1.6011-4(b), Treas. Reg. § 1.6664-2(c)(2).

The Congressional Joint Committee of Taxation Explanation of Code § 7701(o) (JCT Explanation) does provide some guidance as to the scope and intent of this provision.[9] At the outset, it is clear that a court is not precluded from applying the provisions of Code § 7701(o) to traditional leasing arrangements. In this regard, the JCT Explanation provides:

> Leasing Transactions, like all other types of transactions, will continue to be analyzed in light of all the facts and circumstances. As under present law, whether a particular transaction meets the requirements for specific treatment under any of these provisions is a question of facts and circumstances. Also, the fact that a transaction meets the requirements for specific treatment under any provision of the Code is not determinative of whether a transaction or series of transactions of which it is a part has economic substance.[10]

The JCT Explanation also states:

> The determination of whether the economic substance doctrine is relevant to a transaction is made in the same manner as if the provision had never been enacted. Thus, the provision does not change present law standards in determining when to utilize an economic substance analysis.[11]

However, in a footnote to the above-quoted text, the JCT Explanation provides:

> If the realization of the tax benefits of a transaction is consistent with the congressional purpose or plan that the tax benefits were designed by Congress to effectuate, it is not intended that such tax benefits be disallowed. *See, e.g.*, Treas. Reg. sec. 1.269-2, stating that characteristic of circumstances in which an amount otherwise constituting a deduction, credit, or other allowance is not available are those in which the effect of the deduction, credit, or other allowance would be to distort the liability of the particular taxpayer when the essential nature of the transaction or situation is examined in the light of the basic purpose or plan which the deduction, credit, or other allowance was designed by the Congress to effectuate. Thus, for example, it is not intended that

9 *See* JCX-18-10: Joint Committee on Taxation Technical Explanation of the Revenue Provisions of the "Reconciliation Act of 2010," as amended, combination with the "Patient Protection and Affordable Care Act" (Mar. 21, 2010).

10 JCT Explanation, at 153.

11 *Id.* at 152.

> a tax credit (e.g. section 42 (low-income housing credit), section 45 (production tax credit), section 45D (new markets tax credit), section 47 (rehabilitation credit), section 48 (energy credit), etc.) be disallowed in a transaction pursuant to which, in form and substance, a taxpayer makes the types of investment or undertakes the type of activity that the credit was intended to encourage.[12]

Because the reference to targeted tax credit transactions appears in a footnote to the text addressing the relevance of the economic substance doctrine, some practitioners and commentators have suggested that, even if tax credits are not treated as cash, the economic substance doctrine should not apply to a targeted tax credit transaction that is structured in a manner that is consistent with the intent of Congress.[13]

Since the JCT Explanation is neither a House report, Senate report, nor conference committee report, it is not an official part of the legislative history of the new provision.[14] However, other courts have given more weight to explanations prepared by the Joint Committee.[15]

It also should be noted that, in defining types of authority that are relevant in applying the substantial understatement penalty of Code § 6662, the regulations state in part that such authority includes "congressional intent as reflected in committee reports, joint explanatory statements of managers included in conference committee reports, and floor statements made prior to enactment by one of the bill's managers."[16] Separately listed as an additional item of authority is "General Explanations of tax legislation prepared by the Joint committee on Taxation (the Blue Book)." While Joint Committee explanations may not technically constitute expressions of congressional intent, the fact they serve as authority for purposes of the accuracy related penalty under Code § 6662, which is the same section that applies the economic substance codification penalty, would seem to indicate that such explanations should be accorded some interpretive weight.

In subsequent notices, the IRS has provided further guidance for examiners and managers on the application of the codified economic substance doctrine and related penalties and on the definition of "transaction" for purposes of applying the doctrine.[17]

12 *Id.* at 152 n.344.

13 For an excellent and thought-provoking discussion of this issue, see Hershel Wein, "Tax Credit Investments and the Ossification of the Economic Substance Doctrine," The Partnership Tax Practice Series 2016, www.pli.edu.

14 Fed. Nat'l Mortg. Ass'n v. United States, 379 F.3d 1303 (Fed. Cir. 2004).

15 See, e.g., Afaro v. Comm'r, 349 F.3d 225 (5th Cir. 2003); Robinson v. Comm'r, 119 T.C. 44 (2002).

16 Treas. Reg. § 1.6662-4(d)(3)(iii).

17 IRS LB& I-4-0711-015; Notice 2014-58, 2014-44, I.R.B. LB&I-04-0422-0014.

Interestingly, in Notice 2010-62, the IRS stated that "in determining whether the requirements of section 7701(o)(1)(A) and (B) are met, the IRS will take into account the taxpayer's profit motive only if the present value of the reasonably expected pre-tax profit is substantial in relation to the present value of the expected net tax benefits that would be allowed if the transaction were respected for Federal income tax purposes." While this sentence is consistent with the statutory requirement that the pre-tax profit be met on a purely pre-tax cash basis, the very next sentence in the Notice states that "[i]n performing this calculation, the IRS will apply existing relevant case law and other published guidance," which mirrors the statement in the JCT Explanation that "[t]he provision provides a uniform definition of economic substance, but does not alter the flexibility of the courts in other respects." As a result, some practitioners and commentators argued that, even if the economic substance doctrine is relevant, the "credits as cash" approach expressed in *Sacks* still applies in the case of targeted tax credit transactions. Even if this interpretation was adopted, taxpayers were left with the difficult task of determining when a particular transaction was structured in a manner consistent with congressional intent.

12.3.3 Partnership and Partner Characterization Issues

Closely related to the economic substance issue is the need to ensure that tax equity investors will be treated as true partners for federal income tax purposes. In the context of a syndicated Historic Tax Credit transaction, the threshold issue from a tax structuring standpoint is whether the investor will be deemed to be a partner in the owner or the lessee, as the case may be, for federal income tax purposes. This issue can itself be divided into two interrelated questions. The first is whether the entity comprising the owner or the lessee will be considered to be a partnership. The second is whether the investor will be treated as a partner in such partnership for federal income tax purposes.

12.3.3.1 Statutory Definitions of Partnership and Partner

Code §§ 761(a) and 7701(a)(2) define the term "partnership" for federal income tax purposes as follows:

> [T]he term "partnership" includes a syndicate, group, pool, joint venture, or other unincorporated organization through or by means of which any business, financial, operation, or venture is carried on, and which is not, within the meaning of this title, a corporation or a trust or estate.

Code § 761(b) in turn provides that the term "partner" means a member of a partnership.

12.3.3.2 *Culbertson* and Early Case Law

The statutory definition of a partnership has not played a significant role in how the courts have determined whether a partnership exists for federal income tax purposes. The early case law applied a facts and circumstances test to determine whether the purported members of a partnership, in good faith and with a business purpose, actually intended to join together in the present conduct of an enterprise and share in its profits and losses.[18] In its landmark decision in *Culbertson*, the Supreme Court stated that a partnership exists for federal income tax purposes when,

> considering all the facts—the agreement, the conduct of the parties in execution of its provisions, their statement, the testimony of disinterested persons, the relationship of the parties, their respective abilities and capital contributions, the actual control of income and the purposes for which it is used, and any other facts throwing light on their true intent—the parties in good faith and acting with a business purpose intended to join together in the present conduct of the enterprise.[19]

12.3.3.3 Check-the-Box Regulations

In 1997, the Department of the Treasury radically modified the entity classification rules under Code § 7701 to eliminate substantive distinctions between arrangements classified as corporations and partnerships. Under the modified regulations (Check-the-Box Regulations), any "entity" recognized for tax purposes is a "business entity" unless it is "properly classified as a trust under section 301.7701-4 or otherwise subject to special treatment under the Internal Revenue Code."[20] If the business entity has two or more members, it will be classified for federal tax purposes as either a corporation or a partnership. If it has only one member, it will be classified as a corporation or disregarded.[21] An entity that is not classified as a per se corporation has the right to elect whether to be taxed as a partnership or a corporation.[22]

Despite their broad scope and elective nature, to date, the Check-the-Box Regulations have not proven to be of any particular significance in the partnership and partner status analysis in recent cases.

18 Comm'r v. Tower, 327 U.S. 280, 1946-1 CB 11 (1946).
19 337 U.S. 733, 1949-2 CB 5 (1949).
20 Treas. Reg. § 301.7701-2(a).
21 *Id.* § 301.7701-2(a).
22 *Id.* § 301.7701-3(a).

12.3.3.4 The Business Entity Issue and the Sham Partnership Cases

The recognition of an entity as a legitimate separate business entity for federal income tax purposes has been the subject of considerable judicial scrutiny. A number of earlier cases addressed the issue in the context of corporations. In a frequently cited case, the Supreme Court held that a corporation created for a business purpose or carrying on a business activity will be respected as an entity separate from its owner(s) for federal tax purposes.[23] The Tax Court has stated:

> In applying the *Moline* test, courts have looked most frequently to the language following the disjunctive "or," i.e., the business activity of the corporation. Little emphasis has been placed on business purpose. Courts have recognized, however, that *Moline* establishes a two-pronged test, the first part of which is business purpose, and the second, business activity. Business purpose or business activity are alternative requirements.[24]

More recently, the *Moline Properties* case has been analyzed in the context of partnerships rather than corporations. In particular, despite the disjunctive nature of the entity recognition test that was articulated in *Moline Properties*, several more recent cases have interpreted *Moline Properties* as requiring a nontax business need (which is more than a mere business purpose) in order for a partnership to be recognized as a tax entity. This is true even in the case of a transaction that otherwise has economic substance under applicable law. In a series of cases, courts have ignored partnerships as mere shams when tax considerations were determined to be the sole (or at least primary) reason for their existence.[25]

12.3.3.5 Partnership Debt-Equity Cases

Closely related to the sham partnership cases referred to in Subsection 12.3.3.4 are a series of decisions treating the holders of partnership interests with debt-like characteristics as lenders rather than true partners for

---

23 Moline Properties, Inc. v. Comm'r, 319 U.S. 436 (1943).

24 Rogers v. Comm'r, 34 T.C.M (CCH) 1254, 1256 (1975).

25 *See, e.g.*, Merryman v. Comm'r, 873 F.2d 879 (5th Cir. 1989); ASA Investerings v. Comm'r, 201 F.3d 505 (D.C. Cir. 2000), *cert. denied*, Saba P'ship v. Comm'r, 273 F.3d 1135 (D.C. Cir. 2001); Boca Investerings v. United States, 314 F.3d 625 (D.C. Cir. 2003), *rev'g* 167 F. Supp. 2d 298 (D.D.C. 2001), *cert. denied*; Andantech, LLC v. Comm'r, 331 F.3d 972 (D.C. Cir. 2003); Southgate Master Fund, LLC v. United States, 659 F.3d 466 (5th Cir. 2011); Broadwood Inv. Fund, LLC v. United States, No. 13-55626 (9th Cir. 2015); Superior Trading, LLC v. Comm'r, 728 F.3d 676 (7th Cir. 2013); and Chemtech Royalty Assocs, L.P. v. United States, 766 F.3d 453 (5th Cir. 2014).

federal income tax purposes. The most notable of these is *TIFD-III Inc. v. United States*,[26] (the so-called "*Castle Harbour*" case), which is a transaction in which two Dutch banks purported to form a partnership with a subsidiary of General Electric Capital Corporation in an aircraft leasing transaction. Under the terms of the transaction documents, the Dutch banks received preferred returns that resembled interest combined with relatively small interests in profits and losses. The district court rejected an argument by the government that the partnerships were shams and that, even if they were not, the allocations should not be respected. In a series of appellate proceedings, the Second Circuit first reversed the district court on the ground that the interests of the banks were "overwhelmingly in the nature of a secured lender's interest." Later, the Second Circuit rejected an argument by the taxpayer that the interests should be treated as capital interests under Code § 704(e) and, in a footnote, stated that the interests were in fact debt. In doing so, the Second Circuit was not persuaded by a long line of authority advanced by the taxpayer treating pure preferred corporate stock and similar instruments as equity.[27]

Several other recent cases have applied the basic rationale of *Castle Harbour* to deny tax benefits to purported partners whose interests were imbued with debt-like characteristics and whose returns were secured by high credit-quality collateral and other risk limitation devices.[28] Unlike the *Castle Harbour* case, these cases did not involve direct guaranties of a partner's return by another partner. Nevertheless, the courts held that the purported partners were in effect lenders and that the transactions lacked economic substance.

Other cases have upheld true partner status even in a transaction where some of the partners guaranteed a preferred return to another partner. In one oft-cited case, the Tax Court rejected an attempt by the IRS to recharacterize the general partner of a limited partnership (PIC) as a creditor rather than a true partner. Under the terms of the partnership agreement, the limited partners guaranteed that distributions by the partnership to PIC would be sufficient to return substantially all of its capital contribution plus a substantial fixed cumulative return.

26 666 F.3d 836 (2d Cir. 2012), *rev'g* 660 F. Supp. 2d 367 (D. Conn. 2009).

27 *See, e.g.*, Jewel Tea Co. v. U.S., 90 F.2d 451 (2d Cir. 1937); O.P.P. Holding Corp., 76 F.2d 11 (2d Cir. 1935); Lee Tel. Co. v. Comm'r, 260 F.2d 114 (4th Cir. 1958); Comm'r v. Meridian & Thirteenth Realty Co., 132 F.2d 182 (7th Cir. 1942); I.R.C. § 1504(a)(4); Pioneer Parachute Co., Inc. v. Comm'r, 162 F.2d 249 (2d Cir. 1947); I.R.C. § 351(g)(3); Treas. Reg. § 1.305-5(d), Ex. 5; Rev. Proc. 2003-84, 2003-2 CB 1159; Rev. Rul. 90-27, 1990-1 C.B. 50. Note that Code § 704(e) was amended in the TCJA to eliminate the argument advanced by the taxpayer in the *Castle Harbour* case.

28 *See, e.g.*, Pritired I, LLC v. United States, 816 F. Supp. 2d 693 (S.D. Iowa) and Chemtech Royalty Assocs, LP v. United States, 2013 USTC ¶ 50,204 (M.D. La. 2013), *aff'd in part, vac'd and rem'd in part*, 766 F.3d 453 (5th Cir. 2014).

It may have been significant that the guarantee consisted of an obligation by the limited partners to provide funds to the partnership rather than directly to PIC.[29]

12.3.4 *Historic Boardwalk Hall*

The application of the economic substance doctrine and the true partner and partnership factors discussed in the *Culbertson* and *Castle Harbour* cases to a syndicated Historic Tax Credit transaction were addressed in great detail by the Tax Court and the Third Circuit in *Historic Boardwalk Hall, LLC v. Commissioner.*[30] The *Historic Boardwalk* case involved the rehabilitation of an historic building located on the boardwalk in Atlantic City, New Jersey. In the 1990s, the New Jersey Sports and Exposition Authority (NJSEA), which owned a long-term leasehold interest in the property, and New Jersey Casino Reinvestment Development Authority undertook the restoration of the building with the intention of using bond proceeds and their own funds to pay the costs of such rehabilitation. However, after commencing the rehabilitation but prior to completion, NJSEA was advised by a consultant to seek investors interested in the tax benefits arising from the Historic Tax Credit. After a period of negotiations, a subsidiary of Pitney Bowes (PB) agreed to invest in the transaction. Under the negotiated investment terms, PB was admitted to Historic Boardwalk Hall, LLC, a New Jersey limited liability company formed by NJSEA to complete the rehabilitation (HBH), as the investor member. The managing member of HBH was NJSEA. Following completion of the rehabilitation, the building was subleased by NJSEA to HBH for a term of 87 years.

Under the terms of the operating agreement for HBH, PB received a 99.9 percent interest in the profits, losses, Historic Tax Credits, and cash flow of HBH, and was entitled to an annual priority return equal to 3 percent of its capital contributions. Only a small portion of PB's capital contributions was advanced to HBH prior to the placement in service of the rehabilitated building, with the balance dependent and based on the amount of Historic Tax Credits actually allocated to PB. NJSEA provided a number of guaranties to PB, including a construction completion guaranty, an unlimited operating deficit guaranty, a guaranty against environmental liability, and a guaranty that PB would receive the projected federal income tax benefits (including, an indemnification against any loss of such benefits following an audit by the IRS). NJSEA also was granted a right to purchase PB's interest in HBH for an amount equal to the present value of the unrealized federal income tax benefits and cash distributions projected to be allocated to or received by PB during the five-year Historic Tax

29 *See* Hunt v. Comm'r, 59 T.C.M. 635 (1990), where the Tax Court concluded that the guarantee "was based on a payment of partnership contributions . . . and did not constitute repayment of indebtedness. . . . *See also* Investors Ins. Agency, Inc. v. Comm'r, 677 F.2d 1328 (9th Cir. 1982).

30 Historic Boardwalk Hall, LLC v. Comm'r, 694 F.3d 425 (3d Cir. 2012).

Credit recapture period. Following the recapture period, NJSEA had the right to acquire PB's interest in HBH for a formula price equal to the greater of (i) the fair market value of its interest or (ii) any accrued but unpaid priority return due to PB. PB also had the right to put its interest in HBH to NJSEA for the same formula price. The obligation of NJSEA to pay the purchase price under the foregoing options was secured by a Guaranteed Investment Contract (GIC) equal to the anticipated cumulative priority return due to PB.

The IRS challenged the transaction, asserting that HBH should be disregarded as a sham partnership under the economic substance doctrine and that PB was not a "bona fide partner." In effect, argued the IRS, HBH was simply a vehicle by which NJSEA impermissibly attempted to "sell" Historic Tax Credits to PB. The Tax Court rejected the arguments of the IRS and sustained the allocation of Historic Tax Credits to PB, holding that the transaction was not a sham and did not lack economic substance and that PB was a partner in a valid partnership. After considering and discussing the facts of the transaction at some length, the Tax Court concluded that the arrangements had objective economic substance, noting, among other things, that a major purpose of Congress in enacting the Historic Tax Credit was to encourage private investment in projects that, without the incentive provided by the credit, would be unprofitable. In this regard, the Tax Court viewed the credit as the equivalent of cash in applying the pre-tax profit analysis for economic substance purposes. After outlining various other economic risks relating to the investment, the Tax Court also held that the parties had a subjective business purpose for entering into the transaction. Finally, the Tax Court applied the factors in the *Culbertson* case and concluded that a valid partnership existed.

The Third Circuit reversed the decision of the Tax Court but on different grounds. Citing the *Castle Harbour* case and the Fourth Circuit's decision in the *Virginia Historic* case[31] as "guideposts," instead of relying on the issue of whether PB had a legitimate profit motive or business purpose for its investment, the Third Circuit focused on whether PB had a "meaningful stake in the success or failure of the partnership," stating that the fundamental question was whether PB had "any meaningful downside risk" or "any meaningful upside potential" from its investment. In particular, the court determined that the financial projections had been manipulated to create the impression of a pre-tax economic motive by using unsupported and overly optimistic assumptions and that, "in reality, PB could never expect to share in any upside." As a result, the court concluded that the only possible economic benefit to PB, apart from federal income tax benefits, was its 3 percent priority return, the payment of which was guaranteed by NJSEA through the put and call options, and which was fully

31 Virginia Historic Tax Credit Fund 2001 LP v. Comm'r, 639 F.3d 129 (4th Cir. 2011).

secured by the GIC. The court also concluded that PB bore no real risks from its investment, noting that:

(i) with respect to investment risk, PB's obligation to make its capital contributions was contingent upon levels of QREs that would generate credits sufficient to fully cover such contributions;
(ii) with respect to audit risk, PB was fully protected by a tax benefits guaranty; and
(iii) with respect to project risk, most of the project costs were already funded before PB was obligated to make its capital contributions. Moreover, NJSEA had provided both a completion guaranty and an operating deficit guaranty.

The court also was influenced by the fact that the financing available to HBH from other sources was sufficient to fund the rehabilitation without the need for PB's capital investment, noting that the original budget was revised to add a substantial development fee payable to NJSEA and that most of PB's capital contributions were applied to the payment of this fee rather than to what the court viewed as legitimate hard and soft construction costs.

In the end, the Third Circuit concluded that the efforts of the parties to adhere to partnership formalities and to demonstrate economic upside were mere "window dressing" and that in effect the transaction was not a genuine partnership relationship but rather constituted a "prohibited sale of tax credits."[32] Conceding that "[w]here the line lies between a defensible distribution of risk and reward in a partnership on the one hand and a form-over-substance violation of the tax laws on the other is not for us to say in the abstract," the Third Circuit concluded that "after looking to the substance of the interests at play in this case, . . . because PB lacked a meaningful stake in either the success or failure of HBH, it was not a bona fide partner."[33] One interesting aspect of the Third Circuit's opinion was the inclusion of a lengthy footnote in which the court assumed, without explicitly holding, that the transaction had economic substance. However, the court noted: "[E]ven if a transaction has economic substance, the tax treatment of those engaged in the transaction is still subject to a substance-over-form inquiry to determine whether a party was a bona fide partner in the business engaged in the transaction."[34] By expressly declining to address the validity of the "credits as cash" approach in applying the economic substance doctrine, the court permitted the Tax Court's holding on this issue to stand despite its reversal on the partner characterization issue.

---

32 Historic Boardwalk Hall, supra, at 85.

33 *Id.*

34 *Id.* at 50.

12.4 REVENUE PROCEDURE 2014-12

The *Historic Boardwalk* case caused tremendous consternation in the historic tax equity marketplace, largely because of the absence in the opinion of any clear-cut guidelines as to how a transaction could be structured to avoid an IRS challenge to partner status. In response to such uncertainty, on December 30, 2013, the IRS issued Rev. Proc. 2014-12, providing a safe harbor (Safe Harbor) under which the IRS will not challenge partnership allocations of Historic Tax Credits to partners of partnerships that own (or, in some cases, lease) the qualified rehabilitated buildings that generate such Historic Tax Credits.[35] The overall intent of the Safe Harbor was to ensure that a tax equity investor in an historic rehabilitation project shares in both the economic upside potential and the downside risk of loss from such project.

12.4.1 Scope of the Safe Harbor

The Safe Harbor applies in the case of any partnership (a Partnership) that validly claims an Historic Tax Credit. Section 3 of Rev. Proc. 2014-12 makes it clear that, while the IRS will not challenge a Partnership's allocations of validly claimed Historic Tax Credits if the Partnership and its partners satisfy the Safe Harbor, taxpayers should not infer that compliance with the Safe Harbor ensures that the Historic Tax Credits otherwise are valid. In other words, the Partnership still must satisfy all of the technical requirements set forth in Code § 47 (or, in the case of an election under Code § 50(d)(5), Code § 50) for claiming the Historic Tax Credits. Although Rev. Proc. 2014-12 does not explicitly so state, compliance with its terms implicitly confirms the status of an investor as a true partner for federal income tax purposes since a valid partnership allocation necessarily requires that the person to whom the allocation is made be a partner. However, as discussed in Subsection 12.4.3, compliance with the Safe Harbor does not prevent the IRS from challenging the availability of the Historic Tax Credits on some other grounds. A Partnership and its partners that do not satisfy each of the requirements set forth in section 4 of Rev. Proc. 2014-12 do not qualify for the Safe Harbor.

12.4.2 What Transactions Are Covered by Rev. Proc. 2014-12?

Rev. Proc. 2014-12 acknowledges that the partners in a Partnership may include one or more managers authorized to act for the Partnership (referred to in the Revenue Procedure as Principals) and one or more Investors (defined as

35 Note that while Rev. Proc. 2014-12 refers in numerous instances to the allocation of Historic Tax Credits, the IRS has subsequently clarified that, as a technical matter, such credits are not allocated by a partnership. Instead, each partner reports its allocable share of the QREs and calculates the credit at the partner level. *See* Treas. Reg. § 1.47-7 Summary of Contents and the discussion in Subsection 8.1.

partners who are not Principals). A Partnership can be structured as either a Developer Partnership or as a Master Tenant Partnership. A Developer Partnership is defined in section 3 of Rev. Proc. 2014-12 as a Partnership that owns and restores a qualified rehabilitation building or a certified historic structure (a Building). A Master Tenant Partnership is a Partnership that leases a Building from a Developer Partnership pursuant to the terms of a master lease (referred to in Rev. Proc. 2014-12 as a Head Lease) and for which an election is made pursuant to Treas. Reg. § 1.48-4(a)(1) to treat the Master Tenant Partnership as having acquired the Building solely for purposes of the Historic Tax Credit.

12.4.3 What Issues Are Outside the Scope of the Safe Harbor?

Section 3 of Rev. Proc. 2014-12 explicitly states that the Safe Harbor applies only with respect to allocations of Historic Tax Credits. Thus, Rev. Proc. 2014-12 does not apply to low-income housing tax credits, new markets tax credits, or energy tax credits or to state credit transactions. In particular, the Revenue Procedure does not indicate the circumstances under which the IRS may challenge allocations of such other credits or the circumstances under which a transfer of state credits by a Partnership may be treated as a disguised sale under Code § 707(a)(2)(B).[36] Similarly, determinations of whether an expenditure is a QRE and whether a Partnership is the owner of a building for purposes of claiming the Historic Tax Credit are outside the scope of Rev. Proc. 2014-12. Similarly, although not explicitly stated, an IRS challenge to characterization of the Head Lease or any sublease as a true lease for federal income tax purposes appears to be unlikely as a practical matter since, in order to qualify for the Safe Harbor, the lease terms must be commercially reasonable, an issue that is discussed in more detail later. Finally, Rev. Proc. 2014-12 does not address how or if the tax-exempt use property rules under Code § 168(h) apply.[37]

12.4.4 What If a Transaction Involves More than One Type of Credit?

Rev. Proc. 2014-12 does not explicitly state whether, and to what extent, the Safe Harbor applies to a transaction generating both Historic Tax Credits and one or more other federal credits, such as a qualified low-income housing project involving the rehabilitation of a certified historic structure. While the Safe Harbor clearly does not apply to low-income housing tax credits, compliance with the Safe Harbor effectively would at least make it difficult for the IRS to disallow such credits based on a partner status theory. It is hard to see how the Investor could be a partner with respect to the Historic Tax Credit but not with respect

36 In this regard, *see Virginia Historic, supra.*

37 *See* Chapter Seven for a discussion of the tax-exempt use rules.

to the low-income housing tax credits. As a practical matter, this may be a moot point since most low-income housing tax credit transactions are not structured to comply with the Safe Harbor.

12.4.5 Does the Revenue Procedure Provide Substantive Rules?

As is the case with Rev. Proc. 2007-65 (dealing with allocations of energy credits generated by wind facilities) and Rev. Proc. 2020-12 (dealing with carbon capture credits), the Safe Harbor is not intended to provide substantive rules, and no inference should be drawn as to the validity of partnership allocations for taxpayers that fail to satisfy the Safe Harbor. Rev. Proc. 2014-12 emphasizes that the provisions of the Safe Harbor will not be determinative in analyzing partner status in transactions that are outside its scope, nor do the Treasury Department and the IRS intend the inclusion of any particular criterion in the Safe Harbor to be an indication either of their views of the significance of that criterion with respect to any other federal or state tax credit transactions or of whether a partnership has the requisite benefits and burdens of ownership of a building. Section 3 of Rev. Proc. 2014-12 also states that the IRS will not provide private letter rulings to individual taxpayers regarding the allocation of Historic Tax Credits.

12.4.6 Safe Harbor Conditions

The conditions for satisfying the Safe Harbor are set forth in section 4 of Rev. Proc. 2014-12.

12.4.6.1 Prohibition on Separate Investments

Section 4.01 provides that if the Investor receives an allocation of Historic Tax Credits from a Master Tenant Partnership, the Investor cannot also invest in the Developer Partnership other than through an indirect interest in the Developer Partnership held through the Master Tenant Partnership unless such investment is a separately negotiated, distinct economic arrangement (e.g., a separate arm's-length investment in the Developer Partnership to share in allocations of federal new markets tax credits or low-income housing tax credits). Rev. Proc. 2014-12 does not indicate the circumstances under which an investment will be deemed to be a "separately negotiated, distinct economic arrangement," nor does it indicate how large or small an indirect interest in the Developer Partnership held through the Master Tenant Partnership must be to qualify for the Safe Harbor.

12.4.6.2 Nature of Partnership Investment

Section 4.02 sets forth a series of requirements relating to the partnership interests of both the Principal and the Investor.

12.4.6.2.1 *Minimum Interest of Principal*

Under section 4.02(1), the Principal must have a minimum 1 percent interest in each material item of Partnership income, gain, loss, deduction, and credit at all times during the existence of the Partnership. This is consistent with the requirements of Rev. Proc. 2007-65 and Rev. Proc. 2020-12.

12.4.6.2.2 *Minimum Interest of Investor*

Under section 4.02(2)(a), the Investor must have, at all times during the period it owns an interest in the Partnership, a minimum interest in each material item of Partnership income, gain, loss, deduction, and credit equal to at least 5 percent of the Investor's percentage interest in each such item for the taxable year for which the Investor's percentage share of that item is the largest (as adjusted for sales, redemptions, or dilution of the Investor's interest). In other words, in a "partnership flip" structure, if the Investor has a 99 percent interest prior to the flip date, the Safe Harbor would permit the Investor's interest to be reduced to 4.95 percent (5 percent of 99 percent) thereafter. Once again, this is the same approach as that reflected in Rev. Proc. 2007-65 and Rev. Proc. 2020-12.

Although the first example in Rev. Proc. 2014-12 contemplates a "flip" that occurs on a fixed date (i.e., five years after the rehabilitation improvements are placed in service), nothing in the Safe Harbor appears to prohibit a flip based on the achievement of a specified yield target.[38]

12.4.6.2.3 *Bona Fide Equity Investment*

Section 4.02(2)(b) states that the Investor's Partnership interest must constitute

> a bona fide equity investment with a reasonably anticipated value commensurate with the Investor's overall percentage interest in the Partnership, separate from any federal, state, and local tax deductions, allowances, credits, and other tax attributes to be allocated by the Partnership to the Investor.

This sentence initially was the source of some confusion and debate. Some commentators expressed concern that such language may impose a specific pre-tax economic requirement on the Investor. Under this view, the initial "value" of the partnership interest necessarily is determined, in large part, by the amount of equity contributed by the Investor. While the sentence clearly excludes the value of the Historic Tax Credits from this analysis, it is less clear that the initial equity established is ignored when determining the "reasonably anticipated value" of

38 A yield-driven flip was explicitly sanctioned in Rev. Proc. 2007-65.

the interest. Based on public statements by Treasury and IRS representatives at industry seminars following publication of Rev. Proc. 2014-12, it now appears to be clear that the quoted language was not intended to require any particular pre-tax economic return to the Investor. Rather, if, and to the extent that, the Partnership is generating an economic return, the Investor must receive its stated percentage of such return, undiluted by unreasonable fees, rent payments, or other contractual arrangements (examples of which are discussed in Subsection 12.4.6.2.4). This clarification is extremely important since many Historic Tax Credit investments involve community benefit projects such as theaters or museums that will never generate substantial cash returns. Furthermore, it appears clear that an Investor need not receive current distributions of cash flow from a Partnership and may derive a portion of the reasonably anticipated value of its interest from its allocable share of the residual value of the project.

Rev. Proc. 2014-12 goes on to provide that the Investor's Partnership interest will be treated as a bona fide equity investment only if its reasonably anticipated value is contingent upon the Partnership's net income, gain, and loss, and is not substantially fixed in amount. Likewise, the Investor must not be substantially protected from losses from the Partnership's activities. Note the use of the word "substantially" in the context of both the prohibition against a fixed return and the limitation on protection against loss. Practitioners will be required to use their own judgment as to when the "substantiality" threshold is achieved in a particular case. Underscoring this notion, section 4.02(2)(b) goes on to state that the Investor "must participate in the profits from the Partnership's activities in a manner that is not limited to a preferred return that is in the nature of a payment for capital." In short, while there is no absolute prohibition on preferred returns, the reasonably expected value of the Investor's interest must be contingent on the success or failure of the Partnership and there must be a reasonable possibility of the Investor receiving a meaningful cash return in excess of any preferred return. Moreover, as discussed in Subsection 12.4.7.4.2, no preferred return can be guaranteed.

12.4.6.2.4 What Are Examples of Impermissible Arrangements?

Section 4.02(2)(c) provides that the value of the Investor's Partnership interest may not be reduced through fees (such as developer, management, and incentive management fees), lease terms, or other arrangements that are unreasonable as compared to fees, lease terms, or other arrangements for a real estate development project that does not qualify for Historic Tax Credits, and may not be reduced by disproportionate rights to distributions or issuances of interests in the Partnership (or rights to acquire interests in the Partnership) for less than fair market value consideration.[39] This is one of the more problematic provisions

39 Note that section 4.06(4) explicitly permits disproportionate distributions to the Investor to pay preferred returns or to make tax distributions.

of the Safe Harbor. In order to issue opinions that the Safe Harbor conditions have been satisfied, practitioners will need to confirm that any fees, the rent obligations and other terms of the Head Lease, or other similar arrangements relating to the project in question are comparable to those that would be charged or incurred in a project that does not qualify for Historic Tax Credits. In practice, this has required participants in large syndicated Historic Tax Credit transactions to obtain valuation analyses or appraisals to establish compliance with the "comparability" requirement. Reliance on representations from the Principal or the accountants for the project generally have not been sufficient to satisfy Investors and their counsel. Some Investors require that any reasonableness opinion be provided by an independent firm that is not otherwise involved in the transaction. Others will accept a well-reasoned opinion from a division of a qualified firm that is separate and apart from another division or group in the same firm that prepares financial projections or otherwise is involved in a separate aspect of the transaction. The necessity of obtaining third party opinions or analyses has added to the costs of these transactions.

In addition, comparability analyses have been hampered to some extent by an "apples and oranges" problem. In theory, a reasonableness opinion should rely on direct comparables in analyzing fees, lease terms, and other similar arrangements, including an analysis of low, median, and average ranges for comparable fees, rents, and other terms (calculated on a per unit, square footage, or other appropriate measurement approach). However, the unique nature of historic rehabilitation projects often makes this difficult. Development fees are a good example. Traditionally, development fees in historic rehabilitation projects have been much higher than in conventional real estate projects, due in large part to the substantial additional time and effort required to comply with SHPO and NPS requirements. By contrast, development fees in conventional real estate projects typically have been much lower; in such cases, developers frequently realize deferred profits from their development efforts in the form of carried interests and similar arrangements. As a result, finding comparables has sometimes proven to be a challenge.

An even more difficult task has faced experts who are asked to verify that the terms of a Head Lease are comparable to those of a master lease in a transaction that does not involve Historic Tax Credits. In the first place, with certain exceptions, master leases are not common in "conventional" real estate transactions.[40] As a result, compliance with the Safe Harbor requires a comparison of Head

40 These exceptions include the use of master leases to satisfy certain conditions set forth in Rev. Proc. 2002-22, 2002-1 C.B. 733 relating to the treatment of tenancy in common (TIC) interests in transactions intended to constitute tax-free exchanges under Code § 1031. Master leases also have frequently been used to comply with certain rent restrictions applicable to REITs and as a credit support tool. *See* Jonathan Talansky & Jade Newburn, *The Use of Master Leases in Commercial Real Estate Transactions*, The Practical Real Estate Lawyer (Sept. 2019).

Lease terms to something that may not exist in the area in which the project is located. Moreover, the rent and other terms in leases where an election is made under Code § 50(d)(5) (and Treas. Reg. § 1.48-4(a)(1)) necessarily will be quite different from those in a "conventional" lease because of the impact of the credit on the economics and the covenants and other terms designed to ensure compliance with the technical requirements relating to the credits. With the passage of time, sophisticated appraisers and valuation experts have developed methods for dealing with such issues but only at significant additional cost to the participants in the transaction. Typically, reasonableness opinions addressing Head Lease terms identify any available actual master leases in directly comparable (unlikely) or at least similar projects in the geographic area where the Building(s) is located, summarize the terms of such leases, and compare that data to the provisions of the Head Lease. One of the key elements addressed in the analysis typically is the amount of the "leakage" between the gross rent received by the Master Tenant Partnership from its operations and the rent payable by the Master Tenant Partnership under the Head Lease to insure that the Head Lease rent is not unreasonably diluting the value of the Investor's interest.

One other point is worth emphasizing. The IRS has informally stated that the disproportionate distribution test applies at the Developer Partnership level if, as frequently is the case, the Master Tenant Partnership has an equity interest in the Developer Partnership. As a result, it is important to carefully scrutinize the distribution and fee arrangements at the Developer Partnership level to ensure that they do not reduce the value of the Master Tenant's interest in the Developer Partnership or indirectly reduce the value of the Investor's interest in the Master Tenant Partnership by reason of such a reduction in the value of the Master Tenant Partnership's equity interest in the Developer Partnership (which value should be variable based on the economic success of the Developer Partnership and not "substantially fixed in amount").

In the case of a Master Tenant Partnership, section 4.02(2)(c) contains a special rule with respect to a sublease of the Building from the Master Tenant Partnership back to the Developer Partnership or to the Principal of either the Developer Partnership or the Master Tenant Partnership. Such a sublease will be deemed to be unreasonable unless the sublease "is mandated by a third party unrelated to the Principal." For example, if an unrelated lender requires that the Master Tenant sublease the building back to the Principal as a condition of making a loan to the Developer Partnership, the sublease will not automatically be deemed to be unreasonable. The same would be true of a sublease mandated by a governmental agency or, in the case of a hotel or similar transaction, an unrelated franchisor. However, based on the first sentence of section 4.02(2)(c), the terms of the sublease still must not be "unreasonable" compared to the terms of such a sublease in a project that does not qualify for Historic Tax Credits. Accordingly, any reasonableness opinion should address the terms of the sublease. Since the Investor cannot be "substantially protected" from losses from partnership activities and the Investor's return must be contingent on the results of operations and not "substantially fixed in amount," the sublease should provide for variable or participating rent consistent with non-historic rehabilitation transactions. Moreover, whether mandated by a third party or not, the terms of a sublease of the building by the Master Tenant Partnership will be deemed to be unreasonable unless the duration of the sublease is shorter than the duration of the Head Lease. Note that there is no statement concerning how long the "tail" period between the term of the sublease and the Head Lease must be. It also is worth noting that the special rule in section 4.02(2)(c) applies only to a sublease from a Master Tenant Partnership and not to a direct lease by a Developer Partnership to a Principal. Although not explicitly stated, presumably neither a sublease from a Master Tenant Partnership nor a direct lease from a Developer Partnership to a Principal that contains arm's-length terms that satisfy the "reasonableness" standard described here would constitute an impermissible guarantee of partnership distributions under section 4.05(2) of Rev. Proc. 2014-12, discussed in Subsection 12.4.7.4.3. Finally, the Master Tenant Partnership may not terminate its lease of the Building from the Developer Partnership during the period in which the Investor remains as a partner in the Master Tenant Partnership.

12.4.7 When Does an Investor Need to Make Its Contribution?

12.4.7.1 General

Section 4.03 requires that the Investor contribute a minimum unconditional amount (Investor Minimum Contribution) to the Partnership before the date that the Building is placed in service (generally, when the rehabilitated Building is ready and available for use for its intended purpose, as evidenced by the issuance of a certificate of occupancy or similar documentation). The amount of the Investor Minimum Contribution is 20 percent of the Investor's total expected capital contributions to the Partnership as of the date the Building is placed in service. The Investor Minimum Contribution must be maintained by the Investor throughout the duration of its ownership of its interest in the Partnership (and must not be protected against loss through any arrangement, directly or indirectly, by any person involved with the rehabilitation except as permitted under section 4.04(1)). Unlike the provisions of Rev. Proc. 2007-65, the Safe Harbor does not permit the Investor Minimum Contribution to be reduced by distributions of operating cash flow.[41] Contributions of promissory notes or other obligations for which the Investor is the maker are not included in

41 I.R.C. § 4.06(4) appears to provide an exception to this prohibition in the case of preferred returns and tax distributions to the Investor. The scope of the exception is not totally clear since it refers to contrary provisions in the same "paragraph."

determining whether the Investor satisfies the Investor Minimum Contribution. Although the Safe Harbor requires that the Investor Minimum Contribution be made before the placed-in-service date, it does not say how long before. As a result, Investors frequently have been able to protect themselves against most of the construction risk by deferring the Investor Minimum Contribution until shortly before the placed-in-service date. Of course, developers may need equity to fund rehabilitation costs and thus often negotiate for some earlier contributions.

12.4.7.2 How Much of the Investor's Capital Contribution Obligation Must Be Fixed in Amount?

Section 4.04 of Rev. Proc. 2014-12 requires that at least 75 percent of the Investor's total expected capital contributions must be fixed in amount before the date the Building is placed in service. In effect, this section limits downward tax adjusters to 25 percent of the total anticipated capital contributions of the Investor. As a practical matter, this is unlikely to pose a significant problem. Most historic rehabilitation projects come in over budget rather than under budget.

Section 4.04 also states that the Investor must "reasonably expect to meet its funding obligations as they arise." Accordingly, while the fixed portion of the Investor's capital contribution obligation presumably may be subject to the satisfaction of reasonable contingences outside of the Investor's control that are expected to occur (such as the receipt of Part 3 approval), at least 75 percent of the amount of such obligation must be fixed up front and reasonably expected to be made. Moreover, the timing of future capital contributions should not be too closely aligned with the date on which a put option is exercisable to avoid an argument that such capital contribution is in effect a "back door" funded guarantee of the put price.

12.4.7.3 How Are Multi-Building Projects Treated?

One issue that is not addressed is how to apply the Investor Minimum Contribution and 75 percent requirements in large multi-year rehabilitation projects involving more than one building. The references in section 4.03 to the "Building" suggest that the requirement would apply on a Building-by-Building basis. For example, if there are two buildings in a phased rehabilitation project and the Investor's total expected capital contributions are $10 million, of which $5 million is attributable to the Historic Tax Credits generated by each building, the Investor would be required to contribute $1 million (20 percent of $5 million) prior to the placed-in-service date of the first building to be completed and another $1 million prior to the placed-in-service date of the second building. In addition, at least 75 percent of the Investor's total expected capital contributions with respect to the first building would have to be fixed in amount before the placed-in-service date of the first building, and the same test would apply to the second building. At some point, however, this approach becomes impractical if not unworkable. The author is aware of large affordable housing projects involving the rehabilitation of dozens of separate buildings, each of which is a "certified historic structure." In such a case, the application of the Investor Minimum Contribution and 75 percent conditions on a "Building-by-Building" basis presents difficult cost allocation and other issues. One approach would be to treat multiple buildings that are integrated as part of a single project as one "Building" for purposes of these tests, in which event the Investor would be required to satisfy the 20 percent and 75 percent requirements before *all* the buildings are placed in service. Further guidance on this issue would be helpful but, as of the date of publication, there is no reason to believe any such guidance will be provided in the foreseeable future.

12.4.7.4 What Types of Guarantees and Loans Are Permitted?

Section 4.05 of Rev. Proc. 2014-12 limits guarantees and loans provided in connection with an Historic Tax Credit investment and has required changes in certain traditional industry practices.

12.4.7.4.1 Permissible Unfunded Guarantees

Section 4.05(1)(a) of Rev. Proc. 2014-12 provides that the following "unfunded" guarantees may be provided to the Investor:

(i) guarantees for the performance of any acts necessary to claim Historic Tax Credits;
(ii) guarantees for the avoidance of any act (or omissions) that would cause the Partnership to fail to qualify for the Historic Tax Credits or that would result in a recapture of the Historic Tax Credits; and
(iii) guarantees that are not described as impermissible guarantees under section 4.05(2).

Examples of unfunded guarantees permitted under section 4.05(1)(a) include completion guarantees, operating deficit guarantees, environmental indemnities, and financial covenants. It is noteworthy that Example One (discussed in Subsection 12.4.8.1) describes an acceptable guarantee and states that "[u]nder the terms of the guarantee, if the Principal or the Partnership fail to meet their obligations [with respect to the unfunded permitted guarantees], the Investor will be repaid all or a part of its contribution and any costs that Investor has incurred with respect to the transaction." Accordingly, the Investor can be protected against catastrophic problems arising from the acts or omissions of the Principal or its affiliates as long as the relevant guarantee is not secured in some manner and does not contain minimum net worth or liquidity covenants, as described in Subsection 12.4.7.4.2. Notably, the list of permissible guarantees does not include a guarantee or indemnity against recapture resulting from a casualty or condemnation loss, although an Investor presumably is not prohibited from obtaining insurance from an independent third party covering such a loss (including the loss of the Historic Tax Credit).

12.4.7.4.2 What Is an Unfunded Guarantee?

For purposes of section 4.05(1), a guarantee is "unfunded" if no money or property is set aside to fund all or any portion of the guarantee, and if neither the person making the guarantee (the guarantor) nor any person under the control of the guarantor agrees to maintain a minimum net worth in connection with the guarantee. For this purpose, reserves in an amount less than or equal to the Partnership's reasonably projected operating expenses (which presumably include Head Lease rent payments and debt service on Development Partnership loans) for a 12-month period will not constitute an amount set aside to fund the guaranteed amount. Although section 4.05(1) does not explicitly refer to a minimum liquidity (as opposed to a minimum net worth) covenant, prudence would suggest avoiding such a provision.

The prohibition against "funded" guarantees is a direct response to the guaranteed investment contract arrangements in the *Historic Boardwalk* case. The notion that money or property may not be set aside to secure a guarantee is an understandable and workable notion. However, the inability to include net worth or liquidity covenants in guarantees is contrary to normal commercial practice and has proven to be more controversial. Clarification with respect to the scope and intent of the reserve exception also would be helpful. For example, guidance is needed as to how amounts held in a permissible reserve can be applied. For example, must disbursements from the reserve be applied to the payment of operating expenses, or can they be used to satisfy other guaranteed obligations? Once again, as of the date of publication, the IRS has given no indication that any such guidance will be forthcoming soon.

12.4.7.4.3 What Types of Guarantees Are Not Permitted?

Section 4.05(2) of Rev. Proc. 2014-12 addresses impermissible guarantees. Most notably, no person involved in any part of the rehabilitation transaction may directly or indirectly guarantee or otherwise insure the Investor's ability to claim the Historic Tax Credits, the cash equivalent of the credits, or the repayment of any portion of the Investor's contribution due to inability to claim the Historic Tax Credits if the IRS challenges all or a portion of the transactional structure of the partnership. In addition, no person involved in any part of the rehabilitation transaction may guarantee that the Investor will receive Partnership distributions (such as a preferred return) or consideration in exchange for its partnership interest (except for the put right described in section 4.06(2)).

This requirement does not prohibit the Investor from procuring insurance from persons not involved with the rehabilitation or the Partnership.[42]

Similarly, no person involved in any part of the rehabilitation transaction may pay the Investor's costs or indemnify the Investor for the Investor's costs if the IRS challenges the Investor's claim of the Historic Tax Credits.

Finally, no person involved in any part of the rehabilitation transaction may offer a guarantee described in section 4.05(1) that is not an unfunded guarantee described in section 4.05(1)(c).

In short, the Investor must bear 100 percent of the tax structure risk associated with the investment unless it obtains insurance or other protection from a person who is not "involved in any part of the rehabilitation transaction." This represents a major divergence from industry practice prior to the *Historic Boardwalk* decision, although it is consistent with the approach adopted in Rev. Proc. 2007-65 and Rev. Proc. 2020-12. Similarly, no "person involved in any part of the rehabilitation transaction" may guarantee any distributions due to the Investor (whether in the nature of priority returns, tax distributions, or otherwise) and, except in the case of a permitted put option described in section 4.06, may not guarantee any amount due to the Investor under a purchase option or similar arrangement.

Rev. Proc. 2014-12 does not define the term "persons involved in any part of the rehabilitation transaction" or words of like import. Prudence would suggest assuming that such term has a broad scope and would include, among others, any Principal, the lenders, the owners of the underlying land, any major tenant (or, in the case of a Master Tenant Partnership, subtenant), the syndicator (if any), the Developer Partnership, the Master Tenant Partnership (if applicable), any franchisor (if applicable), and any housing agency or other governmental authority serving as a ground lessor (or in some similar direct capacity).

12.4.7.4.4 What Types of Loans Are Prohibited?

Section 4.05(3) of Rev. Proc. 2014-12 prohibits a Developer Partnership, a Master Tenant Partnership, or the Principal of either the Developer Partnership or the Master Tenant Partnership from lending to any Investor the funds to acquire any part of the Investor's interest in the partnership or guaranteeing or otherwise ensuring any indebtedness incurred or created in connection with the Investor's acquisition of its partnership interest. This prohibition is unlikely to have a material impact on Historic Tax Credit investments, although it would be

42 Although Rev. Proc. 2014-12 does not specifically address the issue, logic would suggest that a sublease from a Master Tenant Partnership to a Principal that is mandated by a third party unrelated to the Principal and contains terms that are comparable to those in an arm's-length transaction not involving Historic Tax Credits should not be viewed as some form of "backdoor" guarantee of Partnership distributions. The same logic would apply to a direct lease from a Developer Partnership to a Principal that is not subject to the "third-party mandate" rule in section 4.02(2)(c).

helpful to clarify that if an institution is serving both as a lender and the Investor in a transaction, the fact that a Principal may guarantee the debt will not violate section 4.05(3). In other words, such a guarantee of a loan in the ordinary course of the institution's business would not be deemed to have been "incurred or created in connection with the Investor's acquisition of its partnership interest." A similar issue could arise in the context of certain new markets tax credit transactions involving both loans and Historic Tax Credit equity investments.

12.4.7.4.5 Put and Call Options

Section 4.06 of Rev. Proc. 2014-12 deals with put and call options and has resulted in a significant change in traditional industry practice in Historic Tax Credit investments.

Section 4.06(1) provides that neither the Principal nor the Partnership may have a call option or other contractual right or agreement to purchase or redeem the Investor's interest at a future date (other than a contractual right or agreement for a present sale).

Section 4.06(2) goes on to state that the Investor may not have a contractual right or other agreement to require any person involved in any part of the rehabilitation transaction to purchase or liquidate the Investor's interest in the partnership at a future date at a price that is *more* than its fair market value determined at the time of exercise of the contractual right to sell.

The purchase right provisions of section 4.06 are consistent with those of Rev. Proc. 2020-12 but are very different from those set forth in Rev. Proc. 2007-65, which permitted call options at fair market value but prohibited put options at any price. Several points are worth noting here. In the first place, section 4.06 does not preclude the Principal and the Investor from negotiating a purchase of the Investor's interest in the future upon terms and conditions to be determined at that time, provided there is no commitment to do so at the time of the original investment. Second, it appears to be clear (and IRS and Treasury officials have publicly confirmed) that a put price may be established at even a nominal amount as long as it does not exceed fair market value. The "more than fair market value" prohibition reflects a concern that the Investor would be economically compelled to exercise an above fair market value put option. Finally, some practitioners have raised the issue of whether the prohibition in section 4.06(1) against any call option "or other contractual right or agreement" to purchase or redeem the Investor's interest would prevent the Investor from selling its interest to a third party, subject to a right of first refusal in favor of the Principal to purchase the interest at its fair market value. Read literally, the provisions of section 4.06(1) would appear to preclude such an arrangement.

To ensure compliance with the provisions of section 4.06, the purchase price under a put option should be established as the *lesser* of (i) a stated amount or (ii) the fair market value of the Investor's Partnership interest on the date of exercise, as determined by a qualified independent appraiser, taking into account the provisions of section 4.06(3), which are described in Subsection 12.4.7.4.6.

12.4.7.4.6 What Types of Arrangements May Be Considered in Determining Fair Market Value?

Section 4.06(3) of Rev. Proc. 2014-12 states that a determination of the fair market value of the Investor's interest in the Partnership may take into account "only those contracts or other arrangements creating rights or obligations that meet the requirements of Section 4.02(2)(c) of the revenue procedure and that are on arm's length terms."

12.4.7.4.7 How Are Accrued but Unpaid Fees and Distributions Treated?

Section 4.06(4) of Rev. Proc. 2014-12 makes it clear that the provisions of section 4.06 do not prohibit the payment of any accrued but unpaid fees, preferred returns, or tax distributions owed to the Investor. Read in conjunction with section 4.05(2)(a), section 4.06(4) permits a contractual requirement that such accrued but unpaid items be paid at the time of the exercise of a put option but only the payment of the put price itself may be guaranteed (under an "unfunded" guarantee).

12.4.7.4.8 Abandonment

Section 4.06(5) of Rev. Proc. 2014-12 provides that an Investor may not acquire its interest in the Partnership with the intent of abandoning the interest after the Partnership completes the qualified rehabilitation. If an Investor abandons its interest in the Partnership at any time, the Investor will be presumed to have acquired its interest with the intent of later abandoning it unless the facts and circumstances clearly establish that the Investor did not acquire its interest with the intent of later abandoning it. Some practitioners have questioned how the absolute prohibition on abandonment in section 4.06(5) should be applied to a below-market put option, which clearly is permitted under section 4.06(2). Representatives of the IRS and Treasury have publicly stated that section 4.06(5) was intended to address situations where the Investor intended to "abandon" its interest and report an ordinary (as opposed to a capital) loss on the abandonment.

12.4.7.4.9 Compliance with Code Section 704(b)

Section 4.07 of Rev. Proc. 2014-12 provides that allocations under the Partnership Agreement must satisfy the requirements of Code § 704(b) and the regulations thereunder. As originally drafted, section 4.07 provided that the Historic Tax Credit must be allocated in accordance with Treas. Reg. § 1.704-1(b)(4)(ii) and that, solely for purposes of determining whether a Partnership meets the requirements of section 4.07, the Partnership's allocation to its partners of the income inclusion required by Code § 50(d)(5) should not be taken into account. As discussed in Subsection 9.4.3, in 2019, the Treasury issued regulations clarifying that Code § 50(d) income is not a partnership item that is allocated by a partnership to its partners but rather is recognized at the partner level by the "ultimate credit claimant." Those regulations also modify Rev. Proc. 2014-12 by changing all references to allocations of Historic Tax Credits to refer instead to allocations of QREs and by deleting the sentences in sections 3 and 4.07 that refer to the allocation by a partnership of a Code § 50(d) income increase. In general, the requirement that allocations comply with Code § 704(b) is not a problem. Virtually all syndicated Historic Tax Credit partnership agreements contain provisions that are intended to ensure such compliance.

12.4.7.4.10 Who Is a Related Party for Purposes of the Revenue Procedure?

Finally, section 4.08 of Rev. Proc. 2014-12 states that, for purposes of the revenue procedure, each of the terms "Principal," "Partnership," "Investor," and "person" shall include any related persons. For this purpose, persons are related if they bear a relationship to each other that is specified in Code §§ 267(b) or 707(b)(1).

12.4.8 Examples

Section 5 of Rev. Proc. 2014-12 contains two examples illustrating the application of the Safe Harbor to a transaction in which the Investor invests in a partnership to obtain the Historic Tax Credits. Both examples assume that the tax-exempt use property rules of Code § 168(h) do not apply and assume that the Partnership is validly entitled to claim the Historic Tax Credits arising from the rehabilitation of the Building.[43] Each example describes a syndicated structure that satisfies the Safe Harbor requirements.

12.4.8.1 Example One

In Example One, the Developer Partnership is a limited liability company classified as a partnership for federal income tax purposes. The Developer Partnership is the owner for federal tax purposes of an historical commercial building (Building) that it plans to rehabilitate and thus is treated as the Partnership that must satisfy the requirements of Rev. Proc. 2014-12.

---

43 The description of the examples that follows is substantially identical to the actual text of Rev. Proc. 2014-12. As noted in Subsection 12.4.7.4.9, the IRS has stated that the references in the Examples (and other sections of the revenue procedure) to "allocations" of Historic Tax Credits have been changed to refer to allocations of QREs.

The Principal and the Investor are the partners of the Partnership. The Principal is the manager of the Partnership and authorized to act on behalf of the Partnership. The Investor is an unrelated party that will contribute money to the Partnership in exchange for an interest in the Partnership.

The Investor enters into an agreement with the Partnership to acquire an interest in the Partnership in exchange for an expected capital commitment of \$100×, of which \$75× is fixed. Prior to the date the Building is placed in service, the Investor acquires its interest in the Partnership by making an up-front cash contribution of \$20×. The Investor reasonably expects to contribute the remaining \$80× of its expected capital commitment upon the achievement of mutually agreed upon milestones (e.g., receiving NPS approvals, leasing the Building to tenants).

The Partnership is governed by a partnership agreement that satisfies the requirements of Code § 704(b). From the date the Investor becomes a partner until the date that is five years after the Building is placed in service (Transition Date), the Investor will be allocated 99 percent of the Partnership's profits and losses, as determined for federal income tax purposes. Consistent with the Partnership's allocation of profit and loss, the Investor also will be allocated, and will claim, 99 percent of the Historic Tax Credits [now QREs] available to the Partnership. The Principal will be allocated 1 percent of the profits and losses during this period. As of the Transition Date and until the earlier of the date that the Investor is no longer a member of the Partnership and the date that the Partnership terminates, the Investor will be allocated 5 percent of the Partnership's profits and losses and the Principal will be allocated 95 percent of the Partnership's profits and losses. The Investor has a right to receive a pro rata share of all distributions commensurate with the Investor's share of the Partnership profits. The Investor's partnership interest has a reasonably anticipated value commensurate with the Investor's overall percentage interest in the Partnership, separate from any federal, state, and local tax deductions, allowances, credits, and other tax attributes to be allocated from the Partnership to the Investor.

The Partnership will operate the Building and lease the individual units in the Building to retail businesses under terms that are consistent with lease terms for a real estate development project that does not qualify for Historic Tax Credits. All fees paid by the Partnership, including any fees paid to the Principal, are reasonable and are consistent with fees commonly paid in a real estate development that does not qualify for Historic Tax Credits.

No party involved in any part of the rehabilitation has directly or indirectly provided a guarantee to the Investor regarding the Investor's ability to claim Historic Tax Credits, the cash equivalent of the credits, or the repayment of any portion of the Investor's contribution due to an inability to claim the credits if the IRS challenges all or a portion of the transactional structure of the Partnership. Further, no party involved in any part of the rehabilitation has directly or indirectly guaranteed the Investor that it will receive distributions from the Partnership or that the Investor will receive consideration in exchange for its Partnership interest (other than the Investor's fair market value "put" rights described later). The Partnership and the Principal have provided the Investor with unfunded guarantees commonly provided to investors in commercial real estate development transactions that do not qualify for the Historic Tax Credit. In addition, the Partnership and the Principal have provided an unfunded guarantee to the Investor that the Partnership and the Principal will undertake any acts necessary for the Partnership to claim the Historic Tax Credit. Similarly, the Partnership and the Principal have provided an unfunded guarantee to the Investor that the Partnership and the Principal will not engage in any act that will negatively impact the Partnership's ability to claim the Historic Tax Credit or that would result in the recapture of the Historic Tax Credit. The Principal also has provided an unfunded guarantee requiring it to contribute additional cash to the Partnership to the extent of any Partnership operating deficit. Under the terms of the guarantee, if the Principal or the Partnership fails to meet its obligations, the Investor will be repaid all or a part of its contribution and any costs that Investor has incurred with respect to the transaction. The operating deficit guarantee does not include amounts required to fund expenses for more than 12 months of operations.

Neither the Partnership nor the Principal has any contractual right to purchase the Investor's interest in the Partnership at a future date. For a period of six months beginning on the date that is six months after the Transition Date, the Investor has a put option to require the Principal to purchase the Investor's interest for the fair market value of the interest. The Investor did not acquire its interest in the Partnership with the intent of abandoning its interest.

Under the facts of this example, because each requirement of the Safe Harbor is met by the Partnership and its partners, the IRS will not challenge the Partnership's allocation of 99 percent of the Historic Tax Credits [now QREs] to the Investor.

12.4.8.2 Example Two

In the second example, the facts are the same as in Example One. In addition, the Master Tenant Partnership, a limited liability company classified as a partnership for federal tax purposes, will lease the Building from the Developer Partnership under the terms of a Head Lease. The terms of the Head Lease are comparable to the lease terms of a real estate development project that does not qualify for Historic Tax Credits. The Developer Partnership will make an election pursuant to Treas. Reg. § 1.48-4(a)(1) to treat the Master Tenant Partnership as having acquired the Building solely for purposes of the Historic Tax Credits, allowing the Master Tenant Partnership to properly claim the Historic Tax Credits. Therefore, the Master Tenant Partnership is the "Partnership" for purposes of satisfying the Safe Harbor. The Partnership also will own an interest in the Developer Partnership. The Investor does not own an interest in the Developer Partnership other than its indirect interest held through the Partnership. Further, the Partnership will sublease the Building to retail businesses as described in Example One. The duration of these subleases will be shorter than the Head Lease.

Once again, because each of the conditions to the Safe Harbor is met by the Partnership and its partners, the IRS will not challenge the Partnership's allocation of 99 percent of the Historic Tax Credits to the Investor.

12.5 WHAT IF A TRANSACTION FAILS TO SATISFY ALL OF THE REQUIREMENTS OF REV. PROC. 2014-12?

Most syndicated Historic Tax Credit transactions are structured in a manner intended to comply with the Safe Harbor. However, that is not always the case. Moreover, even in a transaction designed to satisfy the Safe Harbor, some investors request an opinion from tax counsel that the expected tax benefits will be available even if the Safe Harbor is not satisfied. The issue thus becomes whether the status of the investor as a true partner will be respected under existing judicial precedent, taking into account the possible application of the substance over form, economic substance, sham transaction, step transaction, and other similar judicial doctrines.

There is no simple "one size fits all" answer to this question since any analysis of these issues necessarily will depend upon a thorough review of all of the relevant facts and circumstances. It certainly is possible that a transaction could fail to satisfy one or more technical requirements of Rev. Proc. 2014-12 and still be respected by a court applying existing precedent. The Safe Harbor is just that. It is not a statement of what the substantive law is at any point in time. Assume, for example, that a master lease transaction is fully compliant with all of the provisions of the Safe Harbor except that a Principal is granted a call option to purchase the Investor's interest following the five-year recapture period for an amount equal to its fair market value, determined in a manner that complies with section 4.06(3) of Rev. Proc. 2014-12. Would that fact alone prelude a conclusion that the Investor is a true partner for tax purposes and is entitled to the expected tax benefits from the investment? That seems doubtful.

Perhaps the single greatest uncertainty in analyzing a transaction that is not fully compliant with the Safe Harbor is how to apply the economic substance doctrine if there is only a modest cash on cash return from the investment. While the "credits as cash" theory is supported by a number of cases and administrative pronouncements preceding the *Historic Boardwalk* case and the publication of Rev. Proc. 2014-12, it received a singular boost with a 2022 decision by the D.C. Circuit affirming a decision by the Tax Court that Cross Refined Coal, LLC, an LLC engaged in the production of refined coal (Cross), was a true partnership for federal income tax purposes.[44] The activities of Cross were designed to qualify for refined coal production tax credits described in Code § 45.

44 *See* Cross Refined Coal, LLC v. Comm'r, 130 AFTR 2d 2022-5343, 45 F. 4th 150 (D.C. Cir. 2022), *aff'g* No. 19502-17 (T.C. 2019) (bench op.)

Since the sponsor of the project was able to claim only a small portion of such credits in any given year, the sponsor decided to seek investors who were better able to utilize such credits.

After several months of negotiations, two unrelated investors each agreed to purchase an interest in Cross. Under the terms of the purchase agreement, one of the investors was entitled to exit from Cross and receive a prorated portion of its capital if certain negotiated benchmarks were not achieved. Both of the new investors, as well as AJG Coal, Inc. (AJG), the original sole member of Cross, reviewed daily production reports, approved major decisions, and consulted regularly with Cross management. Each of the members made monthly pro rata contributions to cover operating expenses (including items such as payroll, health insurance, and required materials).

Cross claimed approximately $25.8 million of refined coal tax credits on its 2011 and 2012 tax returns, which were allocated to its members on a pro rata basis. In June 2017, the IRS issued a notice of final partnership administrative adjustment determining that only AJG, and not the two investor members, was entitled to claim the credits. In the view of the IRS, Cross "was not formed to carry on a business or for the sharing of profits and losses," but instead "to facilitate the prohibited transaction of monetizing 'refined coal' tax credits."[45]

Cross filed a petition in the Tax Court challenging the IRS position. After considering the facts, the Tax Court held that Cross was a "bona fide partnership" because all three members made substantial contributions to Cross, participated in its management, and shared in its profits and losses. The IRS subsequently filed an appeal with the D.C. Circuit.

The business and operations of Cross were conducted pursuant to the terms of three key agreements. First, Cross entered into a lease with a coal generator to build and operate a coal-refining facility in the middle of the coal generating station. Second, Cross and the coal generator entered into a purchase and sale agreement under which Cross agreed to purchase unrefined coal from the generator, refine it, and then sell it back to the generator for a price that was $0.75 *less* per ton, ensuring that Cross would lose money on each resale while at the same time giving the generator an incentive to purchase refined coal rather than use raw coal. Third, Cross entered into a sub-license agreement with AJG to use its coal-refining technology.

Because Cross lost money on each ton of coal it purchased, processed, and sold; incurred other expenses from operating its equipment and paying royalties to the sponsor; and had no additional sources of revenue, it was impossible for Cross to realize a pre-tax profit from the business. The only way for Cross to realize a profit was to claim refined coal production tax credits that exceeded such costs. Consistent with this business model, the lease, purchase and sale agreement, and

45 *Cross Refined Coal, LLC*, at 6.

sub-license described earlier all had ten-year terms matching the ten-year period during which the activities of Cross could generate such tax credits.

Despite the absence of a pre-tax profit motive, the D.C. Circuit upheld the Tax Court's decision that Cross was properly characterized as a partnership for federal income tax purposes. Based on the Supreme Court's holdings in the *Tower* and *Culbertson* cases cited in Subsection 12.3.3.2, the court noted that the existence of a bona fide partnership depends on two elements: (i) the partners must intend to "carry on business as a partnership," that is, an enterprise "undertaken for profit or for other legitimate nontax business purposes"; and (ii) the partners must intend to "shar[e] in the profits or losses or both," and the partners' interests must have the prevailing character of equity rather than debt. In this regard, citing the *Historic Boardwalk* case, the Circuit Court acknowledged that if "one putative partner is insulated from the upside and downside risks of the business, its interest resembles that of a secured creditor, not an equity partner."[46]

Although the D.C. Circuit's opinion did not explicitly discuss the codified economic substance doctrine in Code § 7701(o), it did rely heavily on the holding of the Ninth Circuit in the *Sacks* case, that "taxpayers may legitimately conduct business activity that Congress has deliberately made profitable through statutory tax incentives—and may do so with no hope of a pre-tax profit."[47]

In its analysis, the court placed particular emphasis on the following factors in determining whether the investors in *Cross* were partners in a bona fide partnership:

(i) whether the conduct of Cross's business activities was designed not to be profitable on a pre-tax or after-tax basis, had no other apparent non-tax business purpose, and in effect was nothing more than "wasteful activity";
(ii) the extent to which the investors bore their proportionate share of the operating expenses of the partnership;
(iii) the degree to which the investors participated in major decisions;
(iv) the extent of due diligence and of communications between the investors and project managers and other investor involvement in the day-to-day business operations of Cross;
(v) the presence of other non-tax motives for seeking investors, such as spreading investment risk over a larger number of projects; and
(vi) the presence or absence of debt-like protections under which funds are "advanced with reasonable expectations of repayment regardless of the success of the venture" rather than being "placed at the risk of the business."

46 *Cross Refined Coal, LLC*, at 9.

47 *Id.* at 12.

In the view of the court, AJG had legitimate non-tax motives for forming Cross and for admitting the investors, including a desire to spread its investment risk over a larger number of projects.[48] As the court noted, "[L]ow-tax entities (like AJG) often use the prospect of tax credits to attract high-tax entities (like Fidelity and Schneider) into a partnership, and in return, the high-tax partners provide the financing needed to make the tax-incentivized project possible." The court also stressed that the other investors, and not just AJG, "jointly controlled major decisions" and made monthly contributions for operating expenses "commensurate with their status as partners."[49]

In arguing that Cross should not be treated as a true partnership, the IRS focused on the impossibility of earning a pre-tax profit and the various ways in which the production of tax credits "permeated every aspect of [Cross's] business model." The court rejected these arguments, explaining that tax incentives like the production tax credits "exist precisely to encourage activity that would not otherwise be profitable" and noting that Cross's business activities had a "practical economic effect," namely the production of cleaner-burning refined coal, which Congress specifically sought to encourage. The court also rejected the view that a partnership is bona fide only if each partner expects to make a pre-tax profit "at some point in time."[50]

While acknowledging the investors were insulated from some of Cross's downside risk, the Circuit Court concluded that, "[b]y and large, [the investors'] fortunes rose or fell with the amount of coal that Cross refined, which made them bona fide equity partners."[51] Because of their substantial equity contributions and commitments to fund operating expenses, the investors "put millions of dollars at risk, in amounts proportionate to their respective ownership interests."[52] In this regard, the Circuit Court pointed out that Cross experienced two shutdowns, during which it incurred almost $2.9 million in operating expenses without generating any offsetting revenue. In their capacity as partners, the investors were liable for, and paid, their pro rata shares of those expenses.

The court explicitly rejected the IRS's argument that the liquidated damages provision alluded to earlier or the sub-lease provisions protecting the investors against minor fluctuations in variable operating costs effectively converted their equity investments into debt, citing the statement by the Third Circuit in the *Historic Boardwalk* case that "a limited partner's status as a bona fide equity participant will not be stripped away merely because it has successfully negotiated measures that minimize its risk of losing a portion of its

48 *Id.* at 11.
49 *Id.*
50 *Id.* at 12.
51 *Id.* at 15.
52 *Id.* at 18.
53 *Id.* at 15.

investment."[53] As already noted, the court also rejected the IRS's proposed analysis, which weighed the amount of capital placed at risk against the magnitude of the expected tax benefits. Once again, the court emphasized that such an approach did not properly take into account the objective of Congress to provide tax incentives to otherwise unprofitable ventures. The court explained that "[w]ithout more, high after-tax profit margins suggest only that the tax credit is a generous one, not that the entities obtaining them are something other than a legitimate partnership."[54]

In the *Friendship Dairies* case discussed earlier, the Tax Court addressed the difference between tax benefits intended by Congress to encourage investment in specific areas and more generic tax benefits (such as accelerated depreciation and the investment tax credit) that are simply intended to encourage investments in capital goods. As the Ninth Circuit and D.C. Circuit recognized in *Sacks* and *Cross Refined Coal*, credits such as the Historic Tax Credit are not generic benefits; rather they are intended to encourage investment in a specific area identified by Congress as being critical to the economy and in effect to transform what might be an unprofitable investment absent the credit to a profitable one. This type of targeted, congressionally mandated, subsidy credit is intended to incentivize socially beneficial investments that otherwise might not be made. Unlike the general investment tax credit in *Friendship Dairies*, the Historic Tax Credit is not merely a proxy for generic depreciation deductions; it is an incentive to make an investment in a limited and specifically targeted area that has been identified by Congress as requiring the incentive in order to achieve the socially desirable goal of rehabilitating historic properties in the United States.

The rationale expressed in the *Sacks* and *Cross Refined Coal* cases appears to apply equally well to a typical syndicated Historic Tax Credit transaction. As was the case in *Sacks* and *Cross Refined Coal*, Congress has specifically created tax incentives for investing in historic rehabilitation projects. That the investor is to obtain, as a substantial portion of its overall return, the tax benefits of the Historic Tax Credit simply reflects the purpose for which Congress created the Historic Tax Credit in the first place. To deny such benefits because a substantial cash on cash economic return does not materialize would appear to be contrary to congressional intent and to the general principle that statutory provisions should be construed in light of their purpose. Moreover, as was the case in *Sacks* and *Cross Refined Coal*, a properly structured syndicated Historic Tax Credit investment has "genuine economic effects" and should not be viewed as a sham. The investor typically makes a very substantial capital contribution to the owner (or, in the case of a lease transaction involving a Code § 50(d) election, the master tenant). There is no payment based on the inflated fair market value of an asset; the amount of the Historic Tax Credit allocated to the investor will be

54 *Id.* at 17.

based on the actual costs incurred in rehabilitating the building(s). The owner or lessee is engaged in a genuine business. Finally, and critically, as was the case in *Sacks* and *Cross Refined Coal*, the transaction has not created tax benefits "from thin air." To the contrary, the transaction will result in the creation of a tangible asset—the rehabilitated historic building—that is consistent with the congressional intent underlying the enactment of Code § 47 in the first place.

Notwithstanding the helpful recent judicial authority, at least in circuits other than the Ninth Circuit and the D.C. Circuit or in any case where unfavorable structuring facts (such as guarantees against risk of loss) exist, the uncertainties concerning the scope and application of Code § 7701(a), which could be interpreted as rejecting the "credits as cash" approach and, even if this is not the case, requires a determination as to how Congress intended a targeted tax credit transaction to be structured, suggests that compliance with Rev. Proc. 2014-12 is the prudent choice whenever possible. The legislative history of targeted tax credits and other similar tax incentives rarely provides significant guidance relating to how the investment should be structured and documented. Of course, an historic rehabilitation transaction in which the tax equity investor also receives a substantial cash on cash return would present an easier case. In any event, the *Cross Refined Coal* and *Sacks* cases both rejected a strict application of the economic substance doctrine in determining partner status and the legitimacy of targeted tax credit transactions and provide taxpayers with powerful ammunition for rejecting an IRS challenge on such grounds.

Finally, it is important to remember that the economic substance doctrine could be applicable not only for purposes of determining whether the investor will be characterized as a partner but also for purposes of determining whether the master lease is a true lease that will support an election under Code § 50(d) (and Treas. Reg. § 1.48-4) to pass the Historic Tax Credit through to the investor (through its interest in the master tenant) by treating the investor as having incurred the QREs arising from the rehabilitation. That is, at least theoretically, a court could find that the master tenant is a partnership and the investor is a partner for tax purposes but, nevertheless, deny all or a portion of the expected tax benefits by refusing to characterize the master lease as a true lease. As a result, an investor who is not relying on the Safe Harbor should nonetheless be prepared to submit evidence that the rent and other terms of the master lease are commercially reasonable and that the lease should be treated as a bona fide lease for tax purposes.

Index